WHAD'YA
KNOW?

- -

Michael

Feldman

WHAD'YA KNOW?

----

a book

Harper Perennial
A Division of HarperCollinsPublishers

The following pieces have appeared in these publications:
North Shore magazine (874 Green Bay Road, Winnetka, IL 60093):
"Gardeners Anonymous," "B.S.: A Matter of Degree," "Reuben, Reuben
(What a Fine World This Would Be)," "Home Improvements," "The No-
Impact Workout (Exercising So's You Don't Know It)," and a version of
"Where There's Smoke There's Ire."
Prime Times (P.O. Box 391, Madison, WI 53701): "Longevity (Living Long Is
the Best Revenge)," "Gardeners Anonymous: A Gardening Fable,"
"Workavoidism," and "Shmex Education."
Isthmus (14 W. Mifflin Street, Madison, WI 53703): A version of "Zen
Judaism Revealed."

First HarperPerennial edition published 1992.

Designed by Barbara M. Bachman

Library of Congress Cataloging-in-Publication Data

Feldman, Michael, 1949–
    Whad'ya Know? / Michael Feldman. — 1st HarperPerennial ed.
      p.   cm.
    Originally published: New York : Morrow, 1991.
    ISBN 0-06-097508-3 (pbk.)
    1. American wit and humor.   I. Title.
[PN6162.F39   1992]
818'05402—dc20   92-52615

92 93 94 95 96 RRD 10 9 8 7 6 5 4 3 2

For Dad:

"It *tuchis* a long time."

Contents

What Do I Know?

They say everybody has a story to tell. Then they go and tell you it. I'd get out now, if I were you. I'd like to say what follows is my story, but if it is, there are more gaps here than in the fossil record, which my story is getting to be. The fact is I'm a middle-aged middle American raised in the middle class who caught the Boomer wave and hence is right on the median on everything, including I-94, the Interstate connecting my Ego to my Id to my Kenosha. We are the rat peristalting through the demographic anaconda, but this too shall pass. And the anaconda will be so fed up it may never swallow another generation.

My only redeeming quality is that I have always felt out of place (and, lately, out of body). As a matter of fact, I wanted to call this "Alien Cohen," my life as a scout here in Wisconsin among the Missouri Synod. I have seen many things, including jar rubbers with Old Testament heroes on them given out by the Aid Association for Lutherans. I have dated Catholic girls and learned names for my sins. I have married out of the faith and never argued about religion, and in it and argued about everything. I have felt the salt spray in my face on a ten-below Madison morning driving behind a salter with my window open due to an inadequate scrape job. What can I say? I have lived.

This then, is my story. Wait—come back!

Look Homeward, Ain'a?

Part One

They say home is where the heart is, but it's more than that. Home is where the heart, lungs, autonomic nervous system, endocrine glands—in fact, all those troublesome, incessantly secreting glands, organs, and nerves are, and it's absolutely the worst place for them, right there where Mom can stem

their flow. Home is where you go in your dreams to check
the mail that's been accumulating all these years and find
that it's still junk and waterlogged besides since someone's
left the flap up since 1965. Home is where, through constant
staring, you have imprinted the wallpaper of your room
upon the circuitry of your chromosones, leaving your DNA
stranded in tiny purple and white geometric patterns not
replicated in nature. Generations to come will blame the six-
ties for this genetic damage, but those of us who were there
know it was the wallpaper, the red, yellow, and blue bal-
loons bumping the ceilings of our mindscapes, and the insid-
ious X-ray shoe machine at Tom's Shoe Store, which, for the
small pleasure of seeing the bones in your feet wiggle,
allowed Roentgen rays to shoot up your little pants legs, setting the stage for the student unrest of 1968.

Home is where you are still confined with your only natural predator, your brother Arthur. Home is what Dad was
always on the verge of losing due to the vagaries of the credit-clothing business, and where you wondered, if he did,
whether you went with it. Home is where the red tiles on
the bedroom floor wobbled because Mother repainted them
by hand while you were up north with Dad the same vacation he let you drive (at age twelve) through the woods and
you piled the '61 Chevy into the very last tree (a good thing,
in retrospect, since the lake was just beyond it). Where, on
rare occasions, Mom would close both kitchen doors, with-
draw a Virginia Slim from one of the sample packs she
amassed downtown while either shopping or returning, and
actually *sit down*, and with her feet up on the seat of a
chrome dinette chair, proving this was still the age of mir-
acles.

Dear Old Dad

Dad was an Oddfellow. When he died, his long-time partner and fellow Oddfellow, Izzy, said that when he (Izzy) went, he wanted to be laid out with the pinochle deck they played with under his lodge sash. As a sixteen-year-old, I was thus confirmed in two beliefs which I hold to this day: loyalty between friends and the likelihood of pinochle in the hereafter.

Dad was born in Kiev but, thanks to the good instincts of his parents, grew up in Vancouver, British Columbia, making him about equal parts British and Yiddish. Thanks to his education at Royal Britannia High School, Dad could recite *The Lady of the Lake* at the drop of a sword. (It couldn't have been Pewaukee Lake, because we sat in that boat for hours and she never showed.) He also preserved in the oral tradition a little ditty called "We're on Our Way to Heligoland" which went:

> *We're on our way to Heligoland*
> *To get the Kaiser's goat.*
> *In a good old Yankee boat*
> *Up the Kiel canal we'll float.*
> *I'm a son of a gun to meet a Hun,*
> *We'll make them understand,*
> *We'll knock the Heligo—*
> *Into Heligo—*
> *Out of Heligoland.*

Needless to say, Heligoland is no more, and I believe the song is why.

Dad was the master of asides. He never said anything over

his breath. In case you missed the punch line, he was not above telegraphing it home with a little behind-the-scenes kick in the pants. Little things. Guns, for example, he referred to as Gentile birth control. He rationalized a fondness for pork chops by saying Mother's cooking rendered them unrecognizable to God. The best stuff (I assumed) started off promisingly enough in the scatological but ended up in the Yiddish. As a result, the only Yiddish I know, I can't use. He used to joke that he would "trade me for a horse and shoot the horse," a *bon mot* which at one time must have had horses rolling in the aisles in the Ukraine.

Since Dad was a CPA, during tax season we hardly saw him at all. In fact, he almost didn't see me, born as I was on March 14, one day before the old filing deadline. I do seem to remember somebody popping in with ledgers under his arms, but it may have just been birth stress. As a child, though, it was a lot of fun tagging along with Dad, that is, if you didn't mind shlepping the briefcase on a surgical accounting strike through Muskego Rendering, or scrambling between the slag heaps at Blue Island Steel hunting down an elusive W-4. Today it would be known as reality accounting.

Dad was a great guy, but he was too trusting: There were always guys who looked like Bud Abbott hanging around the house. There were misadventures: a partnership in a credit-clothing store where a guy could walk in, put five dollars down, and have a nice suit to skip town in. Eventually Dad's partner took the five dollars and skipped. All of us four boys, needless to say, had a surfeit of men's wear, my brother Howard being possibly the only bar mitvah *boy* in a zoot suit. (The long silver watch chain really set off the Torah covers). Dad also dabbled in the stock market, continually surprising analysts by buying high and selling low. He took a bath, too, on the export of clogs to Taiwan, but who knew at the time how that was going to turn out?

Our house was mortgaged so many times, I used to turn in themes written on the backs of promissory notes. (That was only fair, though, since Mother used to keep our diplomas next to the phone to jot down numbers. My National Merit Award had the Roto-Rooter number on the back, which at least made it functional.) Mother's job was to grab the pen out of Dad's hand every time he tried to sign his life away. He always said his greatest asset was Mother, or something to that effect. Knowing Dad, we couldn't tell if he was kidding or not. Considering how much he lost on business deals, she was very nearly his *only* asset. He was a true romantic, though, and used to type Mom little poems on the office Underwood to tenderize a particularly tough piece of steak. I've talked this over with my brothers, and this (the romantic nature, not the steak) seems to be one of those traits that skips generations (unlike, say, baldness and bowlegs). Mother, for her part, always said Dad could have had his pick of women and chose her. As far as I know, this is the only straight line in the Feldman family that was never pounced upon.

On the subject of the opposite sex, I must admit Dad never gave me a "man to man," preferring to let market forces run their course. In fact, Dad gave me only one piece of advice on the opposite sex. I can see him now, sliding down in his favorite easy chair, recently skinned in plastic by mother (significantly lowering its coefficient of friction), and blowing the ashes off the front of his white shirt. "Women," he said. To this day, I've found that to be true.

Middle Age: When pulling an all nighter means not having to get up go to the bathroom.

Home Improvements

I'm at the age where the home-improvement gene kicks in, that innate drive in every man to make his home a castle with drawbridge plans from *Popular Mechanics*. I've always admired the kind of guy who moves into a place and restores it. Thanks to my efforts, the guy who moves into mine will have a chance to do just that.

For several years I've been converting my finished attic into an unfinished one, in an attempt to reduce my assessable value. Once the dust settles there, I've got to redo the living-room walls; what I thought was textured paint turns out to be coffee grounds left in the bottom of the can. The good news on the home front is that the dining-room floor, where I pried off the linoleum eighteen months ago, is much less tacky and the cat no longer sticks to it.

Dad taught me all I know about remodeling by making an example of our house. Our house was like one of the great European cathedrals: never finished. Dad always had a project on the boil, some of which became legends on the block, where he was known as the King of Portland for his visionary use of cement in an attempt to turn our yard into a maintenance-free slab. He would have succeeded, too, if God had intended accountants to know about expansion joints. Instead, the yard buckled and heaved, thrusting jagged peaks of concrete into configurations so like Stonehenge that our yard attracted Druids.

When it came to converting wasted space in the basement,

Dad put the "w" "wreck" room. He transformed a boiler room into the cabinet of Dr. Caligari, using only instinct and materials scrounged from accounting sites. The crowning glory was an innovative suspended ceiling where the pipes were suspended from the ceiling (a technique much in vogue today in public buildings, particularly of a penal stripe). During his "built-in" period he enjoyed considerable success creating the illusion the house had been built around the Zenith console radio, which (after Poe) he concealed in a bedroom wall with only its knobs protruding. The Murphy-bed–inspired ironing board never failed to elicit gasps (particularly when it fell open during dinner), and all four boys slept in drawers modeled after the sleeping quarters on the U-505 submarine at the Museum of Science and Industry.

I can still see Dad and my brother Arthur laughing for hours over a gallon of paint thinner, after which the home projects seemed to get even more ambitious: the garbageman-proof concrete trash bunker, the carpeted garage, and the pastel-block patio which laid to rest Mother's irises. When the paneling craze hit, Dad was among the first to realize its potential, until everyone in the house seemed taller because of the vertical lines.

So when it comes to home improvements, I'm a chip off the old block—which I intend to fill in one of these days with a little Plastic Wood.

I sympathize with the president; I have the most trouble with domestic policy, too.

Shmex Education

Listening to Dr. Ruth, I am struck by the amount of sexual ignorance. Mine. You see, Dad never took me aside, unless it was to remove a smudge from my cheek with a spit-activated hanky. Dad was repressed, I guess. I don't know, he never talked about it. When it came to sex, he was the soul of discretion, referring to parts of the body as Eastern European pastries. Even now, I'm embarrassed to walk into a bakery. When he felt like skirting the issue, he implied that sex was something to get out of the way before marriage. Mother may have gotten it out of the way after. "Sex, shmex," she used to say. This, then, was shmex education.

Not that there weren't resources available to the resourceful: for deep background, the yellowed copy of *The Sexual Habits of Mankind* the folks kept between their mattress and box spring, this being the life work of the traveling Italian sexologist Paolo Mantegazza, who stumbled across nuptial huts the way some globetrotters seem to run aground at just the right bed and board. I don't know what he did for Mom and Dad—there were no drums far into the night—but for me Mantegazza was an early and pervasive influence: When I married, my bride and I were anointed with oil and saffron while burnt offerings were made. In hindsight, I think this may have gotten us off on the wrong foot, but for sheer pageantry it was worth every goat of it.

Woof to the warp of my cross-cultural insights was the clinical evidence gleaned from my brother Clayton's medical books, which fell open, magically, to "Reproduction, Human." It was all Latin to me, of course, and catechism in lieu of Hebrew school was not in the cards. The illustrations, particularly Figure 18-1, were of more than passing interest, but, being cross-sections, they were difficult to reproduce in the field.

School, *in loco parentis*, as usual, begat Hygiene class, the value of which no one who's ever used a washcloth properly can fail to appreciate. The vanguard in the war on puberty, Hygiene class was where gym teachers went when they could no longer spin medicine balls on their noses. The closest we ever steamed to a sexual iceberg was a brush with certain promising vitamins found in tomatoes and said to promote vigor. Since my peers and I were nearly audibly tasseling out as it was, the implications were of little interest. In recent years, though, I've made it policy when ordering a B.L.T. to ask for extra "T." And, for insurance, a side of antelope horn.

⇩

The Frugal Gourmet has nothing on Consuela—I caught her fishing my sweet potato skin out of the garbage after dinner. "My lunch," she said, proud as any angler pulling in a nice striped bass.

The Folks' Saws

You know what they say, folk wisdom is only as good as your folks. Any philosophical rough edges I may have are probably due to the fact that the folk saws in our family had a lot of broken teeth. Even the buzz words could have stood sharpening. When I find myself in times of trouble, what comfort I can draw from my father's sentiments on perseverance: "It *tuchis* a long time *putz* we got there just the same." Maxims like that are why we never got a family crest.

But the fount of wisdom of our genetic pool really flows from Mother. She is a philosopher savant. Mother improves standard epigrams by getting them wrong and somehow still right—"the emperor's nude clothes," for example, or her infinitely more interesting insight into logrolling: "One back scratches the other." Reminds me of her admonition "Do undo others," and the always appropriate "You can lead a horse to water, but you don't want to drink it." The horse sense doesn't end there, either; countless times Mother has inveighed ("oy-vayed," really) against "washing horses in midstream." If you do and drink it then, you're only doing it to spite your mother. On the other hand, "God bless the child that gets up and gets his own."

Mom has her own school of thought that the general public could do a lot worse than to attend. "Just like out of a can" (see following recipe), for example, is her highest culinary award, meaning it tastes good enough to have been mass-produced. (We were raised as Campbell's soup kids, right down to the roses on our chubby little cheeks.) Too, she knows people: "There's good and bad in every group," she likes to note, and if you can't reason with some people, you can always season, which is why she "carries a grain of salt" at all times. Speaking of which, there are the four don'ts: "don't be afraid to ring the meat buzzer" ("they keep the good chickens in back"); "don't start with the neighbors" (*a shonda hopa mit the neighbors*), "don't tip your head" (did she mean "hand," or was it what my brother Howard did?), and the Zen-like "don't ask," the last being almost enough to make you want to have kids just to not answer their questions with it. (Why does a fifty-eight-year-old furrier run off with a girl half his age? "Don't ask.") Even "don't ask" was, often, saying too much: When any particularly sensitive subject was touched upon, e.g., why Frieda's marriage ended sometime during the honeymoon, Mother would jab her finger several times in rapid succession toward the ceiling and, with alarm, whisper the name of Marcie, the all-hearing woman upstairs, in an attempt to prevent her from becoming the all-knowing. For Mom, in her finite wisdom, knows that sometimes the best saying is saying nothing at all.

ADDENDUM:
Mom's "Just Like Out of a Can" Spinach Borscht (Schav)

Admonition: "You gotta eat it good and cold. I leave it in the refrigerator overnight in a quart jar. Use wax paper under the lid so you don't get that taste.

But don't worry: "There's nothing to it. One, two, cee" (a joke).

"First buy a box of frozen spinach. The long kind. Don't get the short." You mean the chopped? "No, don't get it. The chopped. Get the long kind or it won't work. Boil it. You know how to boil water, don't you?—and while it's boiling add some sour salt (they have it at Kohl's), or if you haven't got that a little Realemon is good, not too much (it's strong), and then put in some sugar while it's cooking for the sweet." How much sugar? "Enough for the sour. When it's done boiling, leave it in a bowl and let it cool good. If you don't, when

you add the sour cream, it will curdle." What sour cream?
"The sour cream you add to the spinach when it's good and
cool and put in some nice hard-boiled eggs, sliced."
Shouldn't there be some liquid? "Of course, you add that.
But serve it cold, from the icebox. All the boys liked it. Da-
vey loved my borscht. Just like out of a can."

✔

**Pregnancy: It's lucky that it doesn't happen all at once, like
"Metamorphosis." You know, you wake up one morning and
your wife is on her back, inflated, unable to right herself,
limbs wiggling in the air—that would be a shocker. Or if it
sprang full grown from the father's head, fully clad in
whatever Calvin is showing for spring. My nerves would be
totally shot if there were an egg to sit on—first of all
because Consuela cannot sit still, she's always fidgeting,
stretching, bicycling her legs in the air, definitely not a
setter. On my shift, I'd be afraid to breathe. Probably I could
rig up something in the vanity sink using additional banks of
makeup lights, but I'd worry about her being hard-boiled.**

Holy Mother Church

Mother's taking the Eucharist now; a shocking development in a woman who would come home steaming should some poor soul on the bus have had the audacity to ask if she was getting off at St. Catherine's. True, she spits it out should her daughter-in-law come around (and as a result, should be going to confession, as well) but she wants to fit in at last and I can't blame her (although it is almost impossible to visualize Mom and not hear her mantra "Jewish?" resonating as well). Now she's a leading ecumenical: Not only does she look increasingly like a Native American as she matures, she's gone Transsubstantial as well, and I'm kind of proud of her.

Looking back, I must admit I wouldn't have missed all those years of "us and them," of always being the Indian when we played cowboys and Indians, of hearing how jealous they were of us, when they had the good eyes and the obviously better connections. And the continuing insistence on Jewish girls—what did it get me besides a Jewish girl? Meanwhile, she slips off to a cozy San Jose residential home and takes the Body and Blood first chance she gets. I can't help but wonder what I might have been without the blizzard of clippings sent to me away at school whenever Jews were discovered in China or Ceylon, without Hebrew school when I could have been working on my pivot at second base, and with all the Catholic girls I would have met had she started taking the Host back then—church socials, box lunches in the guild hall, pancake breakfasts filled with them, instead of having to sneak around to CYO dances at St. Theresa's and Holy Angels and trying to drive past the nuns standing under the backboards for a layup (although Catholic girls seemed to like Jewish guys, I think because our guilt came in different places).

Sure, as Catholics we still would have had the Lutherans to deal with, but the odds would have been better, not to mention a galaxy of great ballplayers to look up to, not just Koufax, a Catholic in the White House, and a mind-boggling selection of Irish, Italian, Polish, and Serbian girls (although Sandy Chavez probably still wouldn't have gone out with me), each stopping at a different station of the cross. I might even have been sentenced to Catholic schools brimming with humorous annecdotal material, restrictions to rebel against, demon nuns, lifelong camaraderie, and, yes, girls in plaid skirts and blazers, reflective shoes or not.

But, T. S. Eliot went over late in life, and so did mother—just to be sociable, really, and because the boys who come over with the guitars on Sunday are so cute. Like their mothers, I might add, way back when.

If Newt Gingrich
were cut in half,
which end would
grow back?

Don't Bother Me, I'm Being Sloppily Sentimental

Nostalgia seems to be the inescapable consequence of having a past, no matter how inconsequential. Although it has come to mean a longing for things or times past, the word itself was coined from Greek roots: *nostos*, "a return home," and *algos* "pain," which might refer either to the pain of being away from home or that of returning. Back in the good old days a decent interval was observed before waxing nostalgic, but today, thanks to the fast pace of life, it's not unusual to experience instant nostalgia, or so I still fondly remember just thinking. This hit home the other day when I overheard a kid wistfully recalling the early work of Bon-Jovi. Somewhere someone is thinking back to the Mario Brothers, before they were super.

I'm not immune, although I do manage to stay out of discussions of the Summer of Love (for me it was the summer of Working for the Post Office) and Woodstock, which, at the time, I thought was a lot of trouble to go through for a Sha-Na-Na concert. Had I known Melanie was going to be there,

there's no doubt there'd be a tear in the corner of my eye right now, and a candle in my rain.

I do have a nightstand, however, which is a kind of a time capsule, buried, as it is, in the same soil as our conjugal bed. Every so often I dump out the contents of one or the other and engage in wholesale sentimental associations. Among my souvenirs, if you took the trouble to sift and winnow the receipts, price tags, and plastic sock holders, you'd find: a pen that my late Uncle Abe gave me, inscribed "Stolen from A. Bass"; a tortoiseshell barrette of unknown origin; my John Lennon wire-rims; a quarter flattened on the railroad tracks; my late cat Arthur's front tooth, knocked out in a brawl; Dad's cat's-eye tieclip; a buffalo nickel; a key to an apartment whose locks have long since been changed; a Mount Saint Helens postcard; an aluminum medallion from a bus-station machine stamped MIKE FELDMAN, AGE 9; a Polaroid of my ex-wife's ex-Appaloosa; a rawhide chew from my friend and confidant Rocky; the business card of Juan de la Torres of Santa Fe ("You always have a friend, odd jobs, gutters and downspouts"); a tiny Cracker Jack magic slate; a packet of pansy seeds packed fresh for 1976; a silver pocket watch, broken, of the type once worn by nuns; a New York subway token; a rusting McGovern button; a newspaper article taped to an index card, dated 12/31/51 by my father, describing the removal of the foot of two-year-old Michael Feldman from the basement sewer with a new device called the "Foot Extractor"; a bar chip from the Crystal Corner good for one small drink; a standing-room pass to any Cubs game in 1984; a letter from a collection agency in mint condition; lyrics to a song entitled "Anyone but You" on the back of a Union Cab check stub; a metal bear in a catcher's outfit which clicks; an unwound cassette of Ram Dass; a broken waterbird whistle; a souvenir button from Grandma Prisbrey's Bottle Village in the Simi Valley, California; and a fortune from a Chinese restaurant: "You will save anything."

Why Is This Night Different from All Other Nights?

Passover was an erotic holiday for me, and it had nothing to do with the coming out from Egypt (although reclining can have that effect on you). What it had to do with was the naked-lady glasses pressed into service for the overflow crowd of uncles and aunts and occasional cousin. Dad (a CPA) said he got the naked-lady glasses from a client, although we could never figure out what occupation that would have been. It's true that barter accounted for a lot of the eclectic decor inside our house and out: samovars and brass altar candlesticks from the scrap-metal clients, indoor-outdoor carpeting from the Olefin fiber people, patio blocks from the concrete and aggregate boys, even an ornately framed picture of the Savior from Jesus knows who gracing the garage attic along with several disembodied doors from Clayton's jalopies.

But the naked ladies were special, all six of them, three flesh and three clear. They were objects d'art, not just because my brother Art coveted them, but because they were rendered in a classical style that transcended the trashy intentions of the novelty company that created them. Mother accepted them as sculpture, which, like the reclining nude with the salt and pepper breasts, they were. They were educational, since I had not yet seen real women with bowls of Mogen David on their heads. Sometimes I brought my non-Jewish friends over to admire (but not handle) the sacred glass. "They're for Passover," I'd tell them. "Wow," they'd say, epiphanizing. Several converted, and have our sacred chalices to thank for thriving law practices.

The naked-lady glasses were my favorite ritual objects. They certainly redeemed the bitter herbs and salt water, and the shank bone had nothing on them. If Moses could turn a stick into a snake, I remember thinking, imagine what he could do with a naked-lady glass. True, we might never have gotten out of the land of Pharaoh, but it would have been known as the Golden Age of Stemware. For the transparent Elijah we left a transparent naked lady. Since glasses were raised every few thousand feet during the Coming Out, we encouraged Dad to do the Exodus in real time. By the time we got to the Four Questions, my raised naked lady trembling, it was all I could do not to ask a fifth, "When do I meet something like this?" I stuck to the text, though, and Mom and Dad, thinking the glow in my eyes was spiritual, sold me into five years of servitude in Hebrew school.

Years later I asked my mother for the naked-lady glasses. She said I could have them when, like Moses, I settled down. Two marriages later, she gave them to me.

I don't think Jews can be born again. A makeover, yes. Bankruptcy is close, but it's not the same thing. The upside is we don't have a hell, unless it's Vero Beach in the summer.

Dessert-Errata

A Prayer of Thanksgiving

Go resignedly to the folks' remembering it's just for a few hours. Though you must make appearances at her side as well as your own, eat with as much relish as you can muster, for this, too, shall pass. Choose carefully your words, gingerly stepping around your cousin Ruth's latest fiasco with the Arthur Murray instructor, and ask not about Marlene.

Let on not that you have heard the stories before, and utter them not aloud simultaneously nor anticipate the punch lines. Chew with vigor and bite thy tongue, for the bird hath been cooked since Tuesday, yet praise it tenderly for it never heard a compliment in life. Be sage about the dressing though you know not the origin of the little hard things; should you bite into the wedding band, return it with discretion. Though it resemble syrup, pour not the Manischewitz on the sherbet.

Avoid your Uncle Lou; he is vexatious to the spirit. Kick not your little brother under the table, but show the forbearance of the season and pound him later. Picture Naomi and the kids as alien life-forms, and learn from them. Shout not at Gram, for she heareth what she chooseth. Though you take on much wine, sing not *The Barber of Seville* nor show undue attention to your niece, who has become quite the young lady. If belch thou must, let it not herald the start of a contest. Mince no words over the piece of pie which passeth all understanding.

Above all, say nothing on the ride home, even though the temptation to cite what might have happened but didn't be great. For that give silent thanks, resolving to firm up those plans for Aruba over Christmas.

Amen.

Season's Greetings

Last year I received one Christmas card, from a mortgage company. It showed Santa lowering himself down the chimney, presumably to fore- close. Other than that, there was just the funeral home cal- endar—the one with the mortuary that looks like a branch bank shrouded in snow with the sentimental reminder: "There when you need us."

This year, since I haven't thrown any business either way, I'm not expecting any season's greetings. Starting right after Thanksgiving, I go out of my way to alienate anyone even suspected of harboring my name on a Christmas card list. The campaign has proved so effective, I believe I have reached the point of no return.

Christmas, traditionally, is a trying time of year for me, and was even when I was a kid. First, we had a false fire- place. Second, we were Jewish. Even if Santa had success- fully broken and entered, he would never have gotten past my mother. We did receive our fair share of Christmas cards, but most were from my father the C.P.A.'s clients: Blue Is- land Slag and Smelting, A. Bass Scrap Metal ("Season's Greetings—Top Prices Paid"), and, my personal favorite, Muskego Rendering, which each year sent out a snowy ren- dition of the plant with the legend, "O Come, All Ye Faithful."

Still, the highlight of the season was always the mystery card. Every year my parents got a card from "Sid." Always the same card, NOEL with each letter on a globe ornament hanging from a disembodied fir bough, like White Fang's limb as it reached for Soupy Sales. Inside the card was Merry Christmas in seven popular tongues over a skating rink. It was signed simply, "Sid," in quotes. Nobody claimed to know "Sid," or anyone "Sid" may have stood for, and it was a seasonal bone of contention between Mom and Dad for years until "Sid" slid into the protected realm of folklore like Elijah, the invisible Passover guest.

This year, if all goes as planned, not even "Sid" will be able to track me down. It's just not in the cards; although you never know. They say the "Sids" of the father are sometimes visited on the son.

I miss the Iran-Contra hearings. At the height of the proceedings I sat out in the back with the TV and a case of High Life and chugged every time Colonel North's name was mentioned. Of all the charges that came out of the criminal indictments, I'm most surprised the pantyhose didn't hold up. They were for Fawn, you know. Hers kept bagging out from all the work she was taking home. The biggest remaining unanswered question from the whole affair is, Did Colonel North tell his wife Fawn was overweight but efficient?
Well, mistakes were made. Things came to pass. Beer was consumed on the premises. It happens. The whole mess could have been avoided if Washington had its own baseball team. You know, a healthy outlet. Or if the Contra Aid network had simply sold porcelain clowns on cable, or run a little cubic zirconium.

Husbandry

Part Two

I don't know if opposites attract, but they do oppose. My wife and I couldn't be more different if we tried, which we don't have to. She's a fire sign and I'm water. Together we make a quench. Yes, I know about yin and yang, but it only works on the Korean flag. I'm Robert Yin and she's Loretta

Yang, and we each had our own shows, at one time. I don't know whether it's sides of the brain, or hormones, or which of our fathers filed for bankruptcy first; all I know is when I lived alone there was no question as to which side of the sink was suds and which was rinse. Never was there the slightest hint that the drainer was on the wrong side, let alone that knives should be bundled point up. In those days it was only fitting that opened cans of peaches be stored as such in the refrigerator so as to disturb their original environment as little as possible, and Baggies were not to be recycled, at least as Baggies. If they're coming back, let it be as a higher form of plastic, like a Public Enemy CD.

Now, of course, I realize that a mixed marriage means one between a man and a woman. For us, it's the old story of the ant and the grasshopper, right down to the endless moralizing the grasshopper has to endure for his legendary *joie de vivre*. In my opinion, anybody who can sit on a train track picking his teeth (with a carpet tack yet, flying in the face of oral hygiene and regular professional care) while the 5:09 bears down obviously knows how to "be here now." Sure, an ant can carry twenty times her own weight, fine, as long as she doesn't keep handing you boulders and seriously taking the spring out of your hop.

The President has

ordered the

spraying of

Colombian

broccoli fields.

El Cuento de Consuela

Consuela took to marriage like a duck to oil. We're still getting counseling from the Audubon Society. It was a shock for her, right from the start, taking in what turned out to be a human male and not something with a cute way of walking on countertops. I tried walking on the countertops just to break the ice, but she didn't like it one bit. True, I, too, had some problems adjusting. For the longest time it seemed odd to be shaving one of two faces in the bathroom mirror. Now I draw the line at letting her flush for me, and I've stopped tipping when she hands me a towel, since, after all, her gratuity (50 percent) is figured in.

I feel we've grown. In fact, hand me the tape measure and I'll prove it. More and more we've come to resemble one another and sometimes fight over the ballet shoes. I've learned that "a conversation" is when one person speaks while the other one listens and then responds whenever she's through. ("Are you through?") That you need to reply in some fashion—even a perfunctory "Yes, dear" will do—to every question, even "Did you have fun at the tavern?" (Example: "Yes, dear, we made things out of pipe cleaners and pretzels.") I now know there are two sides to every story, and they're both hers; that a flashing yellow does not mean "step on it" to everybody; and that when the "Don't walk" flashes you're supposed to hop back up on the curb, or, if you're on an island, swim back. "Sharing" is now my middle name. You have to learn how to share, because if you don't she'll take

a bite right out of your hard-boiled egg anyway, grazing
your index finger. (On get-togethers with her family I discovered everybody eats what's in the other's hand, sometimes
biting a Book-of-the-Month-Club selection, or a can of household cleanser. I once watched in horror as Consuela snatched
and devoured the last piece of dill pickle from her blind
Gram. I can still see those poor hands fluttering around the
empty plate like sparrows whose nest has been knocked out
of the eaves with a rake.)

Compromise is the key word—or "compromised," to put
it in the descriptive—even little things like tucking in her
corner of the bed and not yours, so at least somebody can hit
the floor running should the need arise. I gave up sleeping on
the diagonal—if you try it in marriage, you form an X. Unless you can master the basket weave (which I think I saw
illustrated, one time), you'll be much better off teetering on
your brink with the sheets clamped in the vise of *rigor sleepis*
so she can't anchovy-roll on you. Try to minimize the effects
of habits you can't change—maybe your bleeding palms are
stigmata and not the result of her habit of dropping knives
point up in the strainer. Write some things off as inexplica-
ble, like why, when she washes a few things out in the sink,
it's always the same few things, and just brush your teeth in
the bathtub.

I've come such a long way, I feel that my second marriage
has finally prepared me for my first. I guess you're always
one behind. It takes years, after all, to learn about someone
else, and just an instant for your wife to find out about it.
You may think you know the person you marry, but you
don't, not even the parts you thought you had a lock on, like
ethnicity. I, for example, have always been attracted to
Spanish-speaking women because of their dark good looks
and the fact that they don't use possessives. The fact is, I
thought I'd married Spanish. Consuela sounds Spanish,
doesn't it? It does, but she doesn't. She's Jewish. Thirty-five
long years of ginger sidestepping wasted, and for what? A
misunderstanding.

The story is, Consuela grew up—not under, but alongside—liberal parents who permitted her to choose her own
ethnic background. Mamá y Papá gave her a lot of latitude,
and she supplied the longitude. She was Ojibwa for a while,
before walking a mile in the wrong moccasins. But she was
clearly Latin when I met her: the white lace, the single long,
black braid (now hanging alongside my belts), always reading *One Hundred Years of Solitude* in real time. It was impossible to believe she wasn't at least from the Canal Zone. Now
I know the flashing eyes were tearing from her contacts.
When I think of all the pauses I thought charming as she
searched for the right word in English—of course, she did!
Everybody in Sterling, Illinois, does.

It sounds hard to believe, but when she insisted on a rabbi
for the ceremony, I thought she was just thinking of me (a
good sign). Turns out this was the reform rabbi who taught
her Spanish. *Así es la vida!*

A reunited Germany is
probably a good thing, but
somebody should have
made them promise they
wouldn't start calling
themselves "The Fatherland"
again. "The Motherland,"
"The Neuterland," O.K.,
although the latter may
cause some confusion with
the Netherlands. And
whatever happens, no Fourth
Reich. Three Reichs and
you're out!

Batching It

I must be the marrying kind. I can't seem to take more than a decade alone before encasing myself in amber again. The upside is I'm very well preserved and quite lifelike.

I was never much of a bachelor. You would have noticed me had you been up at the rail on one of the few occasions I ventured into a singles bar: I was the one in the parka, looking like I just stopped in to smell the leather. I never mastered the art of small talk; maybe it was my tone or something, but my "What are you drinking, there?" usually got a "What's it to ya?" Even when I was afforded a civil "Harvey Wallbanger," it was usually with such a perfunctory sideways glance (a limited rotation of the sternocleidomastoid that the liquor soothed?—but they couldn't all have sore necks) that it was clearly not worth discussing, let alone escalating into the possible levels of interpretation of the Little River Band's latest. In short, I always felt like leaning over to a woman and saying, "Can I leave you alone?"

Now that I leave the same woman alone, my singular attempts seem like they never happened, which was pretty much the case. Still, on the rare occasions when I'm left unattended for a weekend, I must admit to once in a blue moon slipping out into the nightlife to alienate the young crowd by playing entire Deep Purple CDs on the jukebox, or riveting on a married couple at the bar having an interaction so familiar that, should she excuse herself, I could stand in for her until she got back, were it not likely to be misinterpreted. I am undeniably more approachable, now, though: When I go to the Crystal Corner, say, the young bucks regularly flash me the "V" and say "Peace," respectful of the fact

----

that I'm the one the girls leave their coats and purses with when they get up to dance (sensing, when they smell Bounce instead of Stetson, I can be trusted). Since they never carry more than a few dollars, though (what—does somebody buy their drinks?), there's not really much in it for me, so, once their articles are safely claimed, I put the old hood up and pad my way home to catch the tail end of *Nightline* and maybe bake up a batch of Toll House chips (Consuela's favorite).

President Bush
says, if life gives
you the
Greenhouse
Effect, grow
orchids. As for
global warming,
he recommends
L. L. Bean's Cool-
Weave shirts.

The No-Impact Workout

I used to like to climb a rope in gym, but that, like the Pythagorean Theorem, doesn't come up much in later life. Now my chin-ups are done shaving. Once in a while I get the urge to hold the backs of my ankles and walk around like a duck, but I hardly ever throw the medicine ball around anymore. I can't say I miss the sensation of being rolled thin.

I was the kind of student a gym teacher could hate. I was discouraged by having the wind knocked out of me. Losing did not spur me on. Once I saw that other people were stronger, faster, and more buoyant, I gave up physical humor for mental gymnastics. Now the only horses I vault are in my mind. I was wary of any enterprise requiring a jock strap or, worse, requiring nothing at all, as in swimming at Washington High, the last bastion of the Greco-Roman ideal. Nude swimming among adolescent boys not only does not develop character, it does not develop a backstroke. But you should see my crawl.

I have inadvertently managed to stay in good shape, though. Thanks to nervous tension, I have a comparatively flat stomach, although if I ever relax it'll be all over. Then I'll have to shop for belt buckles at truck-stop gift counters. While I have no regimen to speak of, I shake my head a lot, which seems to keep the levator scapulae in fine fettle. Pacing has done wonders for my calves. For the thighs and lower back, you can't beat the rapid succession of getting up and sitting down on days spent debating whether or not to leave the house. Facial tone, meanwhile, is aided and abetted by the jaw drops when I do get out and discover women are working out as well, and in body gloves.

One thing I'm very careful about is watching my sweet intake, studying each bite of a 5th Avenue Bar before eating, just in case something worthy of litigation turns up in the nougat. I used to watch my starches, but if you've seen one potato, you've seen them all. These days, upon leaving the lunch counter, I'm careful to fill my pockets only with Sweet 'n Low. I've given up salt entirely, resorting only occasionally to licking car tires in winter. In lieu of salad dressing, I just squirt a little lemon in my eye.

Having a mate, of course, is ideal for getting those muscle oppositions going. Not only do Consuela and I enjoy logrolling one another over to the other side of the bed, but we like to stand on either side of a door and push. This works with all doors, although with a revolving one, you run the risk of trapping the shopper in the next wedge over without air. Still, you can't beat it for dynamic tension.

From my hatha-yoga days, I know the importance of breath and make every effort to remember to draw it in. Sometimes it gets a little labored. Ever since I realized that the word *inspiration* comes from *inspiring*, I've tried to inhale more than exhale. I don't know what happens to the difference, but I could venture a guess.

I take very few drugs, except aspirin, and that only in self-defense. Other than that, I drink coffee; I should go with the decaffeinated, but it leaves me lethargic and unable to tremble. And trembling is a great way to work off calories.

Nasal Passages

I don't feel like a forty-year-old. I feel more like four ten-year-olds, each pulling in a different direction. It's not unusual for the one heading south to have more pull. True, I've registered for my male-pattern baldness (Mediterranean), but I figure if I get it shaved into a bat I'll be back in business.

If my copy of *Passages* hadn't been thumbed to death, at least I'd know what I was going through now, if anything. I'm not sure I have the makings of a crisis. True, the image of the girl at the Photomat keeps coming back to me (cropped). It probably doesn't mean anything, though. I mean, she must give double prints to everyone. Then there are the recurring dreams, the ones from which I wake up aroused, thinking I've just secured an 8 percent mortgage with no points. Occasionally I bolt upright in the middle of the night, not merely staring mortality in the face but finding her trying to affix a clothespin to my septum. I blame it on the copies of *Woman's Day* they leave around the Laundromat.

Seems like only yesterday I was having an identity crisis. Or someone was. I think it was me. For years I was beside myself and didn't even know it. Oh, I looked familiar, all right, but I just couldn't place me. This was only compounded by a prolonged postadolescence during which no one could tell me what to do, even though no one tried. And ceramics, what was that? I started making ashtrays about the time everybody quit smoking, although it may have been coincidence. The Zen did me a lot of good, or would have if I had made more of an effortless effort. It's hard to keep picking up after a thousand-petaled lotus, though. Yoga was

----

not my cup of tea, especially the one you were supposed to be able to pour through your nasal passages, what with the bags always clogging. Plus, all that posturing went against my grain, not to mention my groin. Instead of opening up my chakras, I opened up my kishkes. I had an attitude problem: My mantra was "women in leotards."

This time around I'm ruling out in advance any crisis which results in classes at the "Y." Another woman I think I'll leave to another man. Marriage has finally made me realize that I don't have to go out and search for a woman who's totally wrong for me. Besides, I really don't have the time for a proper affair, unless it's on VHS. Some of the other midlife symptoms sound appealing—sudden and uncharacteristic flamboyance, for example—but, face it, what self-respecting Ferrari dealer wants a '79 Zephyr wagon on the lot? Who knows, I may be on the verge of the partial wisdom that comes with middle age. At least I now know that "I grow old. I grow old. I shall wear the bottoms of my trousers rolled" refers to the waistband and not the cuffs.

 According to a poll, 81 percent of the American public think the Bill of Rights is what you have to send in when you buy an appliance. Seventy-three percent agree with the statement "Due process is a hair-straightening solution." Two out of three think that civil liberties are those enjoyed by civil engineers.

The Biological Crock

I feel kind of left out of the dinner conversations. "Julian's having trouble with solid food—was Tiffany the same way?" What can I chip in? Consuela has no problem taking solid food. Absolutely none. Nor do I face their laundry problems: When newborn fathers hear a baby cry anywhere in the restaurant, their milk drops. You can learn things from them, though: I must admit I have never even heard of projectile vomit, at least not with that kind of accuracy (but you know how it is, this guy's kid has the most accurate projectile vomit of any kid). It was bad enough when these guys were going to Lamaze classes and started breathing funny. And what was that all about using paint rollers on their wives? (Intriguing, but you don't want to show too much interest.)

The signs are unmistakable. A guy you've known for years as an impeccable dresser shows up one day with a diaper on his shoulder. I had no idea you were supposed to diaper the father's shoulder (nice to see cloth making a comeback, though). He's haggard, puffy, worried about persistent rashes and the color of nasal discharges. His, that is, after getting no uninterrupted sleep for ninety-seven days. I'm sympathetic to a fault, but if I hear any more about crib back, I'm going to spit up. I already live in dread of dropping in and having the Betacam of the delivery screened between *Sports Illustrated* bloopers tapes. What are you supposed to say—nice point-of-view?

It's not that fatherhood doesn't appeal to me, it does. But

Cosby's already written the book, Ron Howard's made the movie, and Bob Greene's written the columns. Calvin Trillin has frozen his children in an amusing developmental stage about as long as he can without turning into *Family Circus*. It's all been done. There just doesn't seem to be any percentage in it. Naturally, I sometimes see the liquid-crystal display of my biological clock flashing, but that's just a temporary interruption of power. It passes. Besides, although I could handle fatherhood, motherhood eludes me, and Consuela isn't ready to have a child. She's afraid of the sex involved. The real stopper is that each of us is afraid the child would resemble the other and the balance of terror would be upset. Then you get into the quid pro quo of trying to redress the balance, and before you know it, nuclear-family proliferation. She and I belong to the generation that believes we are our own children. We're giving ourselves the things we never had: dance lessons, piano lessons, dirt bikes, and organized volleyball. If we ever grow up, we could turn out to be very well-rounded. People say we're selfish, but we just say, "Nya-nya-nya-nya-nya-nya." In the meantime, it's a fact that shlepping one another to soccer practice can strengthen a marriage.

Cardinal O'Connor revealed he's coming out with an exorcise tape. A great scene the other day when he told Governor Cuomo, "What we have here is a failure to excommunicate."

From Here to Paternity

Author's warning: The preceding piece, "The Biological Crock," does not work as a contraceptive, even when taken internally, as in eating one's words. That's right, we're pregnant. "Crib back" will soon be an overused entry in my working vocabulary, while others like "peace" and "early retirement" will disappear forever. I must admit the thought of having a teenager in 2003 is daunting (should she be allowed to have male holograms in her room?), especially since I had that century penciled in for a nice adobe in Sante Fe, while I could still ballpeen silver. Now the few years between her leaving diapers and my entering them will have to pass for golden. Still, just hearing the baby's racing heartbeat for the first time was momentous—miraculous, in fact, in that it nearly kept up with mine.

I used to think First Alert was an antimissile system (which, in hindsight, we could have used). All that changed at the very moment I turned as blue as the strip. Deep down, though, I must admit to being pretty proud of just how blue that strip was; in fact, for a while, we were leaning toward the name "Cerulean." Pretty, don't you think?

Consuela is thriving and lately always looks like she's consumed several slices of Black Forest torte. (When I discovered the closet filled with bakery boxes I realized why that was.) Had I realized she was a "glower" (long "o," for a change), I would have suggested doing this early and often.

She's a little nonplussed by her changing form, but now at least she knows how I feel (she joined Prange's Bra Club, and that seemed to relieve some of the pressure). Once she got over her initial worry about whether or not she was making a proper blastula (I don't think you can drop a stitch, but I don't know), she settled nicely, if lower, into the water. The only spat we've had was whether or not to put up the ultra-sound picture. My feeling is, bearskin flicks are bad enough; why subject a kid to hearing what "nice buds" they had ev-ery time somebody drops over? We had the sex test, and, according to the genetic screen, I'm a man, my wife's a woman, and the baby's a girl. So, everyone's accounted for. People say, "What about the surprise?," but I'm a firm be-liever in one per customer.

As for me, I've never felt more like a man. I guess it's all the "live ammunition" references from the other guys in the fraternity, who, outside of telling me how much she will hate me by the sixth month, have not been all that helpful. (One told me to return the Betacam, and I did.) When the swagger wears off, though, I find myself staring at the ceiling fan and wondering whether, now that I've been taken reproductive advantage of, I'll be consumed by my mate. (What a fine web we weave when first we manage to conceive.) Maybe it's just having life insurance for the first time. There's a bounty on my head. Funny how mortality isn't any easier to face even when it means a sizable hike in your net worth. When I get the prepartum blues, I worry about "manned obsolescence": I'm convinced Consuela and the fetus, now that they have all the chromosomes they need, have planned a whole new life together (a change of name when we haven't even named her yet?) while I will just go the way of other seed pods, i.e., blown in the wind. Just hormones, I guess.

At the same time, I do have a new and strong urge to pro-vide. I'm so into protecting and defending, I've been carrying a nightstick. Zoning permitting, I could easily set about making a little nest by pushing pebbles into a circle with my snout, or secrete enough calcium carbonate for a cute bungalow. (I've got to stop watching all those nature shows on public TV; after all, it was an intimate look at the wildebeest that got us into this thing in the first place.) Well, a man's gotta do what a man's gotta do. I sent for the Bozo tickets, and have already begun putting money away toward her phone bills. I'm at an impasse over the wallpaper for her room, since a design can imprint upon a child for life. I'm still afraid of pirates, despite having been landlocked most of my life. *Parents' Magazine* (now kept in my underwear drawer) says to provide a stimulating but not too stimulating environment for an infant. Maybe a little mobile of Jewish attorneys; we'll see.

My child will not want. She may not necessarily have, but she won't want. She can have all the things I never had because I still don't want them. She will, of course, recognize immediately who the pushover is in the family, due to the prominent "P" on his forehead, as in Pa. I am prepared to be shamelessly manipulated by my daughter by age two; all I ask in return is an alliance against you-know-who, since you, little Pftatateeta (just the working title), will be the swing vote. As to a permanent tag, I promise you, in advance, she will never put "Estelle" on that document, no matter how good that might make you in the future at coordinating furniture and drapes. We keep going back and forth about this name thing, but it's tough. You don't get this far in life without having made a lot of associations with otherwise appealing female names. I certainly don't want to conjure up the disastrous fishing vacation where I very nearly lowered the anchor rope around a certain ankle every time I call her for dinner. Otherwise, it's a beautiful name.

As far as physical and personality traits, they're beyond my control, or I would have known better than to attach my mother's feet to my father's legs and try to walk on them (particularly with my grandfather's attitude, although Arthur got a lot more of that than I did). The schnozz, greater than the sum of its parts, should skip generations. It's big enough. How this will sort out we probably could approximate with the help of a police artist, but I'm afraid it would look like one of those depictions of what dinosaurs would have evolved into had they lived (eyes as big as Keane's on her side, slick pates on mine).

I am the youngest in my family (another case of babies having babies), so I don't really know what to expect. Once I learn not to take projectile vomit personally and whether or not you're supposed to fold a diaper like a flag (and if so, should it be illuminated at night?), I think I'll get the hang of it. The advantage of having a baby at this point in life is that, for years, I've been laying in a trove of assumptions, misconceptions, and pointless repetitious stories (many of which were repeatedly and pointlessly handed down to me) that I've been longing to pass on to someone who, at least until she learns to crawl, is a captive audience. And isn't that what it's all about?

The government will be requiring new food labels that are more specific. Products will now be labeled "no fat," "low fat," "reduced fat," and "fat, but great personality." Fiber will be categorized "no fiber, low fiber, high fiber," and "mahogany." Actually, the labels themselves are the best source of fiber on many products. Got to eat a lot of them, though.

If Men Could Talk

Archaeological finds in Israel indicate primitive man could do more than grunt. Why this advance has been lost on modern man is not clear. Perhaps because modern woman doesn't want to hear it. Whatever the reason, it's not just dead men who tell no tales. Live ones don't have much to say for themselves, either. That's why it's so hard to tell whether you've got a live one on your hands or not, particularly if he never looked better.

If men could talk, imagine what the walls would hear. They probably could, too, if (1) women wouldn't say "I knew you were going to say that," hard on the heels of an otherwise nice effort, and (2) if they could remember what it was they implied sometime on June 14, 1975, pertaining to her brother, her thighs, or her brother's thighs. A male, when pressed, can recall what a '75 Monte Carlo looked like ("Didn't your brother have a cream Monte Carlo, a 327?") and highlights of the Carter administration, had there been any. He may even recall taking Yoga and Women's Lit during the War Against Male Tendencies, now lost. (You can hold off your male tendencies only so long before they slam you to the mat. I'm not saying that anatomy is destiny, though; if it were, most of us would have pretty short destinies.)

I guess it all boils down to communication, when it doesn't boil away entirely. In my own case (or rather, on it), my wife and I are different sorts of communicators. She tends to be explicit, while facial tics are plenty for me. She expects something called "a response." In my family, we communicated; we just didn't talk about it. Dad took us aside, but, *tuchis* asides were pretty much all we got: *poch in tuchis, kish in tuchis,* an occasional behind-the-scenes *kick in tuchis.* Enough said. Dad was an innuendist, believing that much less could be said through implication than any other way—a beautiful economy leaving much to the imagination. Consuela, on the other hand, comes from a family where motions were made, discussed, and voted on. I can't recall any plebiscites in our household, where it was strictly one man, one vote, and the one man was Father. Mom never stopped talking and Dad never started. Even when he showed me how to pee, it was by example.

He never did tell me about sex, and I still don't believe a lot of what I hear. Consuela, meanwhile, was growing up with the Visible Man and Woman, and, as a result, knows how to get under my skin. A tolerant person, she nonetheless refuses to regard me as a member of a culture deserving evaluation on its own terms, even if those terms be expressed in grunts, mumbles, body language, and odd jobs performed out of implicit concern.

After all, in my male lexicon, reseating the toilet means, "I love you."

I am starting to feel some of the effects of notoriety. As a matter of fact, I had a Letterman-like incident, where a woman moved into my house claiming to be my wife. She pretty much ignores me, so I figure maybe she is.

Babycakes

We can't agree on a name for the baby. Not even the last one. I say the first one gets my last name, she says the only one gets her family name, one of the more amusing puns made at Ellis Island. (I won't reveal the family name unless it's true about the bounty.) It's the reason Consuela has always gone by only the one name, like Charo and Napoleon.

Feldman, on the other hand, has stood the test of time. My father was a Feldman, and his father before him, although I think that's where it may have begun. Before that we seem to have just been filed under "Jews, miscellaneous." Once we had a genealogist look into it, but it turns out most Eastern European municipalities registered their dogs with more care, and apparently none of the early Feldmans was willing to fetch. We probably had a long and illustrious history. Since the Jews and Columbus left Spain at the same time (they heard he was going to Miami, and it was getting to be October), it's quite possible there may have been a Feldman aboard the *Niña* or the *Pinta* (less likely on the *Santa María*) unless Columbus did his own payroll. And Benjamin sounds Jewish—who's to say he didn't change it to "Franklin"? Even the Bible is of little help, since it tells that Terah begat Abram, Nahor, and Haran, but not that Feldstein begat Finestein and Feldman, if that's how it worked. Some hold with spontaneous generation, but I don't think God would play dice with the Feldmans.

Anyway, the recent history has been solid, producing a rainbow of professionals from the tax islands to the islets of Langerhans, all ready to be bestowed on babycakes, once we get her first name out of the way. Consuela favors "Estelle"

while I'd like something more contemporary, like "Arsenia."
She considers the "a" to be too diminutive, even though she
has that ending herself and it certainly isn't as small as it
used to be. So I guess Pftatateeta is out, despite its Third
World redolence (usually a lock on Consuela's imagination).
Looking for roots I pored over a list of Hebrew names, but
they all seem to put a lot on the line: "Hannah," "grace-
ful"—well, we'll see (odds are against, unless it skips generations); "Rebecca," "captivating beauty"—which nobody told
the Rebeccas I went to school with; "Sarah," "princess"—re-
dundant; "Bat Sheva," "daughter of an oath"—on the
money, but legal-sounding and too close to "daughter of an
oaf" anyway; or "Dikla," "date palm"—never, not on your
frond.

"Molly" is versatile because, like "Michael," it can pass
for Irish. It was high on Consuela's list, but I have an aunt
Molly and I don't want to confuse my mother any further.
There are already three "Roses" creating a bramble in the
family thicket, plus she thinks the Pekinese of one of them
(my brother Arthur's Rose) is her own baby son "David," my
father's name and also that of most of the males of the current generation.

Today I go to the library for a list of nonsense syllables.
And a Croatian dictionary, just to be safe.

Women are so
feminine again it's
getting hard to tell
them from
transsexuals.

The Continuing
Cuento
de Consuela

In pregnancy, Consuela has found her life's work: eating for the benefit of another. She always was a good eater, but never before was there a higher purpose. What's truly marvelous is that the baby likes all the things she does, even those horrible fried (in rapeseed oil) squares of bean curd, although the kicking does seem to increase on these occasions. I can't bear to think there might be a little human with my tastes trapped in there being force-fed hummus on Ak-Mak crackers, but, if so, maybe she'll develop an immunity.

Sleeping is already a thing of the past due to the chain reaction: When the baby kicks her, she kicks me. My guess is this phenomenon stops short of breast-feeding, so there's no pot of gold at the end of the rainbow.

Still no agreement on a name, although we both like "Caledonia," if the song would only die down once and for all. Until then we really can't risk "what makes your big head so hard?"

■ ■ ■ ■ ■

The best thing about winter is seeing other people besides Consuela wearing earmuffs. She wears them on breezy days, year round, because she has small openings. True, I bought her the earmuffs, but only because she used to walk around with toilet paper in her ears, and the ends would always flap, which, by the way, is how she toured Europe, where, she reported, the toilet paper does not seal nearly as well.

■ ■ ■ ■ ■

We inherited a dishwasher in our new home and Consuela swears by it, although it's so loud I just see her lips moving. I don't get why an hour and five minutes of deafening roar is better than fifteen minutes of hand-washing, but it is. Figuring the savings over twenty years, my hands should last nearly three months longer than the rest of me.

■ ■ ■ ■ ■

Consuela, six months pregnant, claims her butt was always this big. Unless I'm losing my grip, she's wrong. She is getting pretty big, though: I had to cook Thanksgiving dinner because she couldn't get close enough to the stove to do it. Lucky she's double-jointed and can fry eggs behind her back.

■ ■ ■ ■ ■

Plans are proceeding for her parents to come down and help for a couple of months after the birth: code name Normandy II. Thank God it's a girl, because the cute little dress that grandmother and mother wore is *de rigueur*.

■ ■ ■ ■ ■

It looks like cloth as opposed to Pampers. The sigh of relief is from the environment, not yours truly.

Saint Bob of the Weeping Woodwork

Ill never forget the day the crew came in and took Bob Vila and stacked him at the curb. I nearly dropped the four-by-eight Sheetrock I had balanced on my head. Suddenly, I was all alone in the home-improvement jungle with the ceiling falling in on me and the walls that had seemed half finished now, glaringly, half torn out. It was like talking to the walls, and asking them whether to fur out or power-nail right to their studs. What about the vapor barrier? The trim? Sobbing uncontrollably (for it is all right for a home repairman to cry), I was thankful Bob had advised the waterproof board.

I hadn't realized it, but I was as dependent on Bob as Anglophiles are on Alistair Cooke and his Victorian garage-sale set. *This Old House* filled a void in my life which coincided with the space my house occupied. True, it was hard to keep up, since they kept changing houses on you, but I rested easy, knowing my trilevel Victorian saltbox with rustic timbers and Doric columns would one day be a very rich archaeological site. Some guys will have a few beers and watch a ball game; I would crack a couple of High Lifes and watch Bob make dream homes come true. Bob could make a room expansion look so easy it was impossible to resist getting out the hammer and loosening a little plaster on the unsightly wall separating the living room from the bathroom. It was easy to forget the shows weren't done in real time. It seems as if the guys came in, poured the floor, knocked up the walls, and at least got the roof trussed out in twenty-seven minutes, but, looking closely, you noticed that by that time the homeowner's glasses had gotten a little thicker and his hair a little thinner, and that his wife, who had been prying out lath with a crowbar, like a good sport, had disappeared altogether. No one said home improvement would be easy. Certainly not I, standing there ankle deep in plaster, needing another six-pack after the friendly little clarinet theme had played (too soon, too soon!), wondering how grasshoppers (*Insects in Love*, on most of these PBS stations) could be mating at a time like this. The crew never arrived, Norm was not in the next room rigging up some cabinets, the wife would be home in an hour to a breezier bathroom than she had left, but still, somehow, I knew Bob would make it better next week. When I heard he wouldn't be back, I was so depressed I hung up my stud finder and called in professionals.

I had lost the will to home-improve.

Glamour says intellectual men are in in the nineties, citing Ted Danson, Robert Redford, and Ron Silver. Nothing like putting a pretty face on an ugly tendency. I would have had higher hopes if they had pointed to Marlin Fitzwater, John McLaughlin, and Pat Buchanan. I guess the idea is that today's women are turned on by committed men. Yes, but will you still care about the rain forest tomorrow? The real test will be to see if *Glamour* changes to a quarterly journal.

...And Gasp!

I'm failing breathing class, and I'm worried because without it, they won't let you have a baby. Everybody else but me can breathe. I don't know how they do it. How can you relax with everyone patting your tummy and telling you "Your life will never be the same" and "Boy, they're a lot of work," with only about half adding "but they're worth it." Not to mention the horror stories in class: the woman who kept saying "I nearly died" with the same smile a man might have (not this one) saying "Yeah, ran her off the road, flipped her three times, and landed upright with the beer still in my hand." Hearing about strange women's stools is unsettling enough (although my ears did involuntarily prick up on the question of whether hemorrhoids retreat as well as advance—the glacial theory), without the harrowing tales. The woman with the breech, whose doctor, in righting it, held on to the fetus and turned *her* upside down. The husband who, while his wife was in labor, went out for Chinese. The woman who backhanded her mate across the birthing room for telling her to imagine she was on a beach when all she could conjure up was a high-cut suit and stretch marks.

As a result, my "in, one, two," stretches to "ten, twelve" before I realize I'm not taking in any air and loudly gasp for breath like a drowning man no one in the room would save. (The men wouldn't dare cross their wives at this point.) She, of course, I add with pride, breathes perfectly and can even alternate nostrils without pinching, a natural Kundalini (but we always knew she had control). Of course I believe it's worth it, but, in those quiet stretches when I should be respiring, I do sometimes examine my own family in that

light, and, I must say, I can't entirely believe we were. I
think my folks should have lived a little! Instead of conceiv-
ing Clayton (it would have been around New Year's, 1936),
why not wing off to Rio? In June of '38, in lieu of Howard,
why not France, beating the heat and crowds of jackbooted
German tourists? Superseding Arthur (Happy New Year
again, dear, 1943), a steamship cruise, where the romance
and intrigue that Arthur never would provide stalk Dave and
Gerry Feldman all the way to the Lesser Antilles and back,
and then, when they tired of traveling, they could just have
started me (1948—June—The Washington Park Lagoon?).

    . . . And Gasp!

 I've decided to have my
house frozen cryogenically
until a cure can be found. As
a starter house, it's finished.
I've already spackled the
walls so often I feel like a
mud wasp. Well, they say a
man's home is to spackle. A
lot of it is having the right
tools. In my case, they don't
make 'em. I've just about lost
the will to home-improve. It
takes so long to get anything
done; one day of work
followed by a week of
regaining partial use of the
affected appendages.

Concerns Shared

Part Three

Let's face it, life is subjective. It depends on your point of view. Somewhere someone is standing on a star looking at our gutters. Naturally, he'd be fascinated, since drainage, as we know it, would not be a possibility on a star. That's my point. You've made it for me.

Why do eyewitness accounts of a crime differ so greatly? Because some people, understandably, had their eyes closed and their fingers in their ears the entire time. If everybody heard sounds the same way, there could be no Julio Iglesias, and a tree would fall in the forest only if he were under it. Even in the retina of the eye, one woman's cones are another man's rods, processing the same images so differently that it's no wonder you can't agree on what to watch on TV, especially since it's unwatchable to begin with.

Give an infinite number of monkeys an infinite number of typewriters, and one will write Shakespeare, all right, but he'll give all the good roles to chimps ("Is this a banana I see before me? Come, let me clutch thee!") even though Lear clearly calls for an orangutan. Meanwhile, in row 3,147,642, third from the back, is a jumpy little squirrel monkey touch-knuckling a Hermes portable and making these "chee-ack! chee-ack!" sounds almost as if he knew what he was doing. What follows was discovered in his "out" box. It is reproduced here because, as primates, even if we see things a little differently, we share many of the same concerns.

I saw a survey
where about half
the kids asked
thought that
World War II came
first.

Hello, I Love You, Won't You Tell Me Your Name?

You have to feel bad for guys in their twenties. Not only do they have to put up with Herman's Hermits on the radio at work (the format known as "Our Music for the Rest of Your Lives") but now I read where the forty-year-old silver-backs are poaching their available females, luring them with condos, health clubs, and incomes their age and better. Many young women seem surprisingly willing to trade a lean solar plexus for a new silver Lexus. In our day we didn't trust anybody over thirty, but not because we thought they'd steal our chicks. I guess we should have thanked our lucky Aquarian stars that straight hair, headbands, and Indian-bedspread skirts were not suitable for business entertaining.

You can't really blame a forty-year-old man who's put off marriage so long his sperm count is in danger of being reported along with the whooping cranes. He could pick on someone his own size, but that would be like taking his work home with him. No, what he wants is the very embodiment of the values he rejected back when their embodiment didn't look so attractive.

It can't be entirely easy for these couples. How are they going to watch *Saturday Night Live* together without Dennis Miller driving a wedge between them? Will she know enough not to call "I Heard It Through the Grapevine" the "raisin song"? What happens should she catch an eyeful of what Dave Clark looks like today? While it's true that Dockers can be very forgiving, will she be able to forget the 501 button flies she has known? Can she bite her tongue should he adopt a modified Zero Mostel hairstyle? Will his drug experience in college and hers in grade school prove compatible? Where would she really like to see his sideburns end? Is there any hope he will be able to resist cross-referencing key dates in "The War at Home" to her teething or taking of solid foods? Will she be driven to tears on hearing "When I was your age I was being tear-gassed in Romantic Poetry?" Will he be able to wear boxer shorts (even Calvin Klein's) and not look like an accountant with his pants down? When the work shirt that's "older than she is" finally disintegrates in the laundry, will he carry the shreds around like a blankee? Will she be forced to listen to "Tommy" until she is deaf, dumb, and blind? How will he continually rationalize his material success to someone who feels no apologies are necessary?

Stay tuned in.

What a Fine World This Would Be

A study at Brandeis should have grade-school boys and girls singing "Reuben, Reuben" across the country. It concludes that boys should not be allowed in the same classroom as girls because they hamper the girls' growth, and suggests they be admitted to school only after reaching the threshold of "emotional and physical stability." Well, maybe you can lead a thirty-five-year-old man to P.S. 47, but you can't make him sit. After all, a guy gets pretty long in the leg by the time he's emotionally stable.

Of course, it's no secret boys hamper girls' growth. We've been at it for years. I assume it's part of the gender system of checks and balances intended to prevent the female from climbing the next rung of the evolutionary ladder alone. I hadn't realized, however, just what a drag we had become until reading that a Professor Mortrude of St. Cloud has implied that girls could be probing the very origins of consciousness were it not for the boys behind them sticking their shoes through the seats.

Girls are, on average, two years ahead of boys, or just entering fiscal 1994. Developmentally speaking, girls, with their propensities for the arts, languages, and insightful thinking, are Renaissance and better, whereas boys are late Neolithic. Girls tend to use more of the right side of the brain, the side where everything that's right comes from. Boys are limited largely to the reflex actions of the cerebellum, allowing them to make surprisingly realistic belches. Girls have sophisticated motor control, permitting them to master folk dances at the drop of a hat, while boys move only when threatened with a rolled wet towel. During the formative years, boys like to be physical in dramatic ways, a tendency modern schools have taken into account with windows which don't open. Creative powers differ as well: Given macaroni, glue, and construction paper, boys inevitably glue the noodles to girls. There's even a memory gap: Girls have complete recall, as boys soon discover.

Girls continue to outpace boys until about the seventh grade, when, ironically, they begin to pay attention to boys. Some girls regress at this point, and have been observed turning in language-arts themes written entirely in eyebrow pencil. Seizing the moment, boys pick up the slack, learn to feel their way around a dance floor, and begin the search for females to hamper throughout their adult years.

We need a more consistent national policy on the environment. Reagan said trees cause pollution; then Bush goes out and plants them. That's why Reagan was always chopping wood—trying to get rid of the polluters. They have trees in Bel Air, but they're too well-bred to release gasses into the atmosphere. It's the gardeners you have to watch out for.

B.S.: A Matter of Degree

The American Council on Education reports it's possible to buy a bachelor's degree for about eight hundred dollars from any one of nearly three hundred diploma mills across the country. Makes me sorry I paid retail. I figure my B.S. cost me fifteen thousand dollars, or will, if I ever get around to that National Defense Loan. Imagine, the equivalent of a like-new Taurus (loaded) for a document I've never been asked to produce. I had nearly completed my master's when I realized they'd never ask to see that, either, and ran out to graduate school with the leeches still attached. Now I see that empty frame on my wall could be filled with a master's for twelve-fifty (post-paid) or a doctorate for twenty-three hundred, thesis defended. I'm no saint, but at these prices I could be a Doctor of Divinity.

The federal government has taken an ambiguous position on diploma mills, having prosecuted some and invaded the Caribbean to preserve others. The Education Council does offer some tips for consumers who naïvely believe they can have the benefits of a college education without being hounded by alumni foundations for the rest of their days. Beware if the application, for example, recommends closing the cover before striking, or asks you to draw a pirate. Should a diploma be offered as part of a package deal—say with live sea monkeys—it may be bogus. Any prospectus asking the make and model of your car may not supply the sheepskin you were hoping for. The educational consumer should also look askance at offers of college credit without any academic requirements, unless you have been recruited into a bona fide athletic program. Vigilance is called for, too, when solicited by "look-alike" schools whose names, at first glance, appear to be those of respected institutions: Near Miss, Eva Braun University, Sonny Tufts, The Electoral College, Cornell Wilde University, Gloria Vanderbilt, Quaker State, Boston Pops University, Votre Dame, and the very nearly prestigious William and Harry, to name just a few.

For consumers on the other end of the stick, that is, those seeking professional services from someone with dubious credentials, verification is not always easy, since it may not be possible to remove a degree from the frame and smear the signatures by the time your lawyer returns from pitching a weeping elder citizen out the door. You can, however, test your attorney's college background by taking him to lunch and daring him to drink a pitcher of beer without using his hands. Should you suspect your family practitioner has studied under Dr. Seuss, take a minute of the forty-five or so you'll have waiting in the freezing examination room to smell his credentials. If there's even a hint of mimeo fluid, hike 'em up, quick.

 The kids of baby-boomers were taught to question authority, but they wouldn't listen.

Beam Me Up

Sex sells, as NASA, trying to stimulate flagging interest in its planned space station, has discovered. A spokesman for the Ames Research Center in Mountain View, California, the agency in charge of creature comforts for the long stays of months or even years on board the space station, says they expect the "normal, healthy professionals" on board to have "normal, healthy sexual appetites." Finally, a trickle-down from the space program worth looking into.

The people at Ames have a team of psychologists, engineers, and architects working right now on the problems of orbital intimacy, using a wealth of data gathered from the cockpits of commercial airliners. In Houston, they're putting couples on the centrifuge. Most report feeling closer than they have in years. Still, there are bound to be complications in orbital sex. Microgravity could raise false hopes. Astronauts themselves may not make the best lovers—who wants to hear a checklist during foreplay? A lot of women don't like a guy who needs a mission specialist in Houston to tell him when to fire his retrorockets. What about the heat shield? Will it hold during reentry? Romance, so crucial to the success of the mission, could suffer when, instead of a playful trail of lingerie and stockings, you would be dodging the rubber anti-g drawers and fluid-collection devices floating in your love nest. Even if they lick the fireplace problem, Harvey's Bristol Cream through a squeeze bottle may not have the same effect.

Afterward, there's the very real problem of drifting apart, even as you share a pull on a tube of anchovy paste. Should he roll and pitch over and become just so much more space

junk (leaving her to vacuum up her tears), the resulting friction might negatively impact on the mission, particularly if
she refuses to share data with him for thirty or forty orbits
or, worst case, should he extravehiculate and she change the
airlocks. Hard feelings would be inevitable, as well, among
other crew members who have to be content with biological
experiments of the frog kind.

Crucial will be the counseling provided the postorbital
couple during the natural letdown once back on earth. After
all, several million pounds of thrust will not easily be forgotten.

➤ I've decided to take no
heroic measures to promote
my health. Consuela and I
have agreed to be test
cases; she will shop at the
co-op, exercise, stay away
from electromagnetic
sources, ingest bee poop
and other homeopathic
sources, and I will continue
to live the way I have. The
survivor gets to say "I told
you so."

You Should Live So Long

Longevity isn't what it used to be. The Bible says that before the Flood man lived to an average age of nine hundred and twelve years, nine hundred ten if he smoked. After the Flood, man's stock plummeted to three hundred and seventeen, showing the degree to which the Creator had tired of His Creation.

Secular investigation reveals that prehistoric man lived to age eighteen and died from a blow to the head. Today, thanks largely to improved nutrition, an eighteen-year-old is merely stunned by a blow to the head. Since that time, life-spans have crept upward. Though they crammed in a lot of living, Vikings were pretty much plundered out by twenty-three. In the Middle Ages, ironically, very few people were, since thirty was pushing it. Life expectancy in New England in 1789 was thirty-five point five years, a fact not lost on the Founding Fathers, who set the minimum age for the presidency at thirty-five to promote turnover.

Statistically, Scandinavians live longer than anyone except Frenchwomen. Americans live longest in the states with the fewest distractions; South Dakota, Minnesota, Iowa, Kansas, and, the winner in the long run, Nebraska, where a woman who isn't seventy-four isn't trying. On the other hand, a man in Arkansas is as good as dead. Americans, it turns out, could live a year longer if they moved to Canada, but would find magazines slightly higher.

Clergymen outlive athletes, but college graduates die like everybody else. The average married man lives two thousand and five days longer than his single counterpart, but cannot recall a single one of them. According to Metropolitan Life, life-insurance policyholders live two and one half years longer than the uninsured, or, as fate would have it, nearly exactly the time it takes to earn the premiums.

Sure I know what
opened-ended
mutual funds are.
That's when I buy
them and the
bottom falls out.

Faith to Faith

I always thought there was a lot of charm in the notion of man as a pinch pot God breathed life into, especially since I did ceramics for years without one of mine coming to life. They did, however, multiply and become fruitbowls. What I never could see was the Divine six-day work week. Fortunately, He was off the other fifty-one. The idea of God creating man in His own image, though, has to be blasphemy. I'm not sure I could believe in a God with fallen arches and (concurrently) high insteps, that little additional curve of the spine which makes the belly appear to protrude, and lactose intolerance. Then there's the Chosen People thing. Sure we were chosen, but for what? On balance, it's been an honor we could have lived without. Maybe the Lutherans would like it, or the Unitarians.

Man is a religious animal, much more so than, say, the iguana, or even the praying mantis, which likes to make a show of it. It seems to be his nature to grapple with moral questions, usually within forty-eight hours of the incident. The questions seem fundamental, like the one everybody else keeps asking about you—why are you here? Do right and wrong apply to me? Where are the Jewish televangelists offering careers in law, medicine, and accounting if you just call this number? Man asks the questions and religion supplies totally implausible answers, which, the way things are going, are probably true. This, then, is faith.

This is not to say that much of what appears in the Bible does not reflect cultural biases. The notion that woman was made from man's rib, for example. I've made some good ribs, but never one that started telling me about herself and what I could do to help. That would win the cookout, easy. Women get a bum rap for sin as well, simply because they are the one sex to whom a reptile would open up. Adam had been eating the apples all along (hence, Adam's apple) and knew they were naked the whole time. He liked it. They probably were shown the door to Paradise because Adam was keeping another rib on the side. It's tough to stop with just one.

Philosophers have argued the existence of God for eons. One of these days He may be forced to break up the argument in a dramatic fashion—involving, say, lava, vermin, and possibly boils for good measure, just like in the good old days. To prove the existence of God it would be necessary to build a God trap, but, being all-knowing, He's not about to step into it. Some point out that the Divine in "the Divine Miss M." had to come from somewhere, but the simple truth is faith has to be taken on faith, like a cosmic "Because I Said So." Still, there are answers to many questions if you just don't think too hard about them:

Why do we have to die? Why do leaves have to die? Why do we have to rake them up when they do? Why is there fifteen-minute parking downtown when it takes that long to cross the street? Simply stated, God has the inventory, He's got to move it, and the lot is only so big. Besides, what is it about you that you think should go on forever?

Why doesn't God intervene anymore? He doesn't want Charlton Heston to work. Besides, He's got a lot more kettles whistling than just ours—creating universes where opposites repel, for instance, and where plaids and stripes go together. Maybe He's working on a Bigger Bang (for the Buck) theory, or something so large even He can't lift it. Could be He's just trying to figure out where He put his gravitational lenses so He can see what's going on.

If there's a Supreme Being, how can there be evil? That's like saying if there's a refrigerator, how can there be dirty fingerprints on it? Somebody put them there, and ate the rest of the tuna fish, too. This is not a theological problem; this is your problem.

Is there an afterlife? This life isn't hard enough, you want to live without public transportation or ice water? The sad truth is, there is no afterlife and there's not much happening at the moment, either. Maybe he who has the most two-for-one dinner coupons at the end does win after all. (I would check expiration dates.)

Does God hear my prayers? God hears everything. Unfortunately, He hears it all at the same time, so it sounds like an Italian restaurant with a tin ceiling. As a result, you may get the Chicken Vesuvio without praying for it.

Is there a Hell? There used to be, but they put in a mall and now nobody goes.

Are there angels? Yes, dancing on the heads of pins, however, has enfeebled them; now many now have the heads of pins. They're flighty and easily mistaken for moths. Guardian angels *will* watch over you, but they won't do anything. That's a different union (Teamsters).

Is one religion better than another? Of course. Yours.

Zen Judaism Revealed

I am, by nature and inclination, a Zen Judaist. Zen Judaism, an unorthodoxy, is a fusion of the wisdom of the east with the confusion of the west side of Milwaukee, 2718 N. 58th Street, to be exact. A Zen Judaist believes not only in a God the Father or a God the Mother, but in Mom and Pop Gods, never completely reconciled opposites who move the world along in fits and starts because each has His or Her own way of doing things. For example, She creates flowers and ornamental shrubbery; He, lost in His own world, comes up with His pride and joy, an ox ("It's strong!" He tells Her. "Like I don't know what!"), which, unfortunately, makes its debut in her flower garden. He spends the better part of an eon secreting a rugged pinnacle out of pure testosterone and pluck, while She has been summoning forth—not to be mean, but because She has to get water to Her trampled flowers—rushing torrents, which wear away His mountain and result in an annoying song by Donovan to boot (a completely unforeseen outcome). Like the yin and yang of the Buddhists, they are a team pulling in opposition. Somehow the cart manages to skid along the bumpy road with its wheels pointed out.

As a result, the only prayer a Zen Judaist has is to get out of the house, naïvely thinking that he can get out from under the samsaric wheel. The realization of Irony, the tent pole of Zen Judaism (for the Zen Judaist the opening of the fifth eye, since he already has four), occurs when he finds his mate and soon discovers that being at sixes and sevens is the way

of the world. Then and only then has he achieved *tsoris*, the
Buddhist *satori*, a steady diet of aggravation which, nonetheless, produces results, even if they mostly resemble her.
Moreover, the Zen Judaist *mensch (Bodhisattva)* now can't
help but perceive the duality within himself; he cannot hic-
cough without saying, "Hi, Mom," or sneeze without thinking, "How you doing, Dad?" His soul mate, too, is such an
obvious combination of her mother and father it doesn't
bear bringing up, particularly to her. Thus, the Zen Judaist
has gone back to the wellhead, drawn up the bucket, and
put his back out of commission for two weeks. So it is in
heaven, where, on the seventh day, the Mom and Pop Gods
vowed they would never again take on such an ambitious
project without an architect.

The Supreme
Court ruled
against
➤ protection for the
religious use of
hallucinogens.
Looks like Mogen
David 20-20 is out
for Passover.

Chanukahmas?

Christmas can be a trying time of the year for interfaith couples. Unless one of you can force the other to convert, it pays to show a little sensitivity toward the other person's traditions, no matter how much pagan mumbo jumbo they seem to be. Holiday traditions mean a lot to people, particularly people in retail, so if yours is a mixed marriage (by that I mean two different religions, not a marriage between a man and a woman), here are some tips:

1. Remember, neither the Old nor the New Testament records lightning striking a house just because it had a Christmas tree. But, just in case, ground it. (I would avoid large replicas of beef cattle in gold or fiberglass, though, unless you're living above a Cal's Roast Beef.) If a Christmas tree gives you problems, just hang little dreidels on it and think of it as a marketplace of ideas. And since there's usually a star on top anyway, so it has six points? As to the type of tree—compromise, get a yew. Do try to keep in mind that a Jewish spouse coming home to a wreath on the door is subject to cardiac arrest, and then you'll need two wreaths on the door.

2. A crèche is pretty hard to disguise, even if you call it a lawn ornament. But try it—and put out a couple of deer as well, and maybe a reflecting globe. You might follow the example of some town halls that have avoided legal challenges to their crèches by putting a cutout of a Jewish pediatrician in with the baby. (The miracle then becomes the fact that he makes house calls.)

3. Strings of lights around the house are pretty easily

explained, since you're on the approach to the airport anyway. Just tell your spouse it'll lower your Homeowner's.
Stockings next to the fireplace won't generally raise the
hackles of a Jewish mate unless they're stuffed with rosar-
ies. Hard candy is always nice. Another tip: Use support
hose. His mother did. Don't push your luck and expect
your Jewish spouse to get up on the roof to install a ply-
wood Santa and reindeer, however. Jesus, after all, was
the last Jewish carpenter.

4.   As for holiday music, why not meet each other half
way with Barbra Streisand doing "Little Drummer Boy,"
and the Mormon Tabernacle Choir version of "Yentl"?
"Chestnuts Roasting On an Open Fire" is also a nice
choice because Mel Torme could be Jewish. A word to the
Jewish spouse: They can't *make* you go to the "Sing-Along
Messiah," and since you don't know the words or the tune,
a good case can be made for leaving you at home. If you
do go, don't worry if everybody gets all worked up. If they
light torches, worry.

5.   Relax about going over to your spouse's family for
your first Christmas. You'll come back. And you'll be a met-
ric wrench set and a pair of sorrel boots richer. Remember,
to your non-Jewish spouse, "exchanging presents" does not
mean returning them to the store. At least not right away.
Christmas cards should be in good taste and two-dimen-
sional. They should never say "One of us wishes you a Merry
Christmas," but, rather, something seasonal, such as "Cold
enough for you?" If you are celebrating your first Chanukah,
don't buy scented candles or light beer by mistake. ("I said,
'Festival of Lights,' not 'Bud Light.'") Don't worry if at first
the significance of the holiday escapes you; the miracle of
the oil lasting eight days in the temple will soon take on
meaning as you try to stretch the few dollars left in your account after celebrating both holidays.

They Poll Herefords, Don't They?

I'm the Yancy Derringer of data: I clip polls from the paper and keep them under my fedora, just in case I ever have to pull a figure out of my hat. Should we be sitting around playing sheepshead and the debate turns nasty over who sleeps more, where, for example, I can push over the card table for a shield against flying fish crackers while—with lightning speed—producing from somewhere on my person figures which clearly indicate that 75.2 percent of midwesterners do (say the polyurethane mattress people), sleeping seven hours a night, compared to only 68.5 percent of westerners (more of whom are likely to have gotten up to go to the bathroom, since 36 percent have more than one, double the number in the nations's heartland (Kohler and Kohler). This chills things out and order is quickly restored.

I originally developed the poll reflex because of my ex-former father-in-law, whose data always seemed to indicate 99.9 percent, whether it was the percentage of marijuana smokers going on to heroin or the fat in the roast his wife was setting before him. Avogadro had his number, and R.B. (not his real initials) had his. Some years back, when the government of Haiti said 99.9 percent of the electorate endorsed the regime of Baby Doc, I was sure R.B. had turned up in Port-au-Prince. Anyway, just to prepare for family get-togethers, I loaded up on polls in areas that were likely to come under contention (these were, after all, the seventies) with every intention of thrusting them under his nose. I never did because I knew it wouldn't work—he'd just say 99.9 percent of all polls lied—but a preoccupation was born and lives still.

Polls, after all, can point you in the right direction, particularly exit polls. The numbers can keep you in touch with the culture, although it's hard to look at leotards the same way once you realize that 45 percent of those who wear them never work out in them. (They may simply be people who think their outline is the inline of the universe.) You begin to dread the previously welcome words "comes with the salad bar" once you realize that 60 percent of the population has committed an "act of slobbery" at a salad bar—"eating in line, sneezing beneath the guard, dipping fingers in dressing or picking food up with the fingers, removing and/or replacing food items," or even teasing their hair over the sprouts. You don't know what to think when you learn that 58 percent of Americans who smoke in bed think it's very risky. But you find reassurance, as well, in the face of critics who believe the American mind is closing, when, in fact, 55 percent of Americans—well over half—know the sun is a star, and by a three-to-one margin rate chicken a better value than college tuition. And how can the work ethic be dead when the Roper people report that only half of the American public feel work interferes with their leisure? Nor can introspection cannot be a lost art when nine out of ten yuppies, according to Lou Harris, find their preoccupation with "self" to be "singularly unattractive."

From facts and findings domestic bliss can be culled as well. A study by a University of Maryland psychologist, for example, confirms that not only do happily married couples today need space, they need about seven hours to cover it, since marriages in which the partners live in different cities are one-fifth as likely to end in divorce as those that thoughtlessly fling bride and groom into the same time and space (which, elementary physics should tell us, two bodies were never meant to occupy). Couples raising children during pit stops ignore the collective wisdom of Walt Disney World at their peril, since the Epcot poll reveals that 84 percent of parents think parents are too lenient, a finding that may be skewed due to the respondents' having just spent thousands to shlep the whole ungrateful lot to a Magic Kingdom where privileges may not be revoked. (Even so, only 9 percent, according to Harris, would have used genetic engineering to make their children more agreeable on long van rides.) Thirty-four percent of the children, by the way, think kids are treated too leniently, but you can bet 99.9 percent of them mean the little squirts who keep unwinding their Metallica tapes.

What bugs me about the census is that I finally get two toilets and they don't ask. Of course, one's just sitting on the porch, but it really beats wicker. I must admit I reverted to old test behavior on the census and just made a pattern with the circles. Plus, I filled in "Pacific Islander," because I thought they'd be undercounted.

Making Amotivation Work

Part Four

I have Amotivational Syndrome, or would, if I could maintain it. It's really not such a bad thing when you consider how many things are not worth doing. I don't believe in the Protestant work ethic. Why should I? I didn't get the nose. The Jewish work ethic runs in my family; it just ran out

when it got to me, the dregs of the gene pool. When I priori-
tize, everything comes out on the bottom. I have many of
the attitudes most often associated with great wealth. Unfortunately, I don't have the money. *Noblesse* without the
oblige. I can't get excited about making a modest income, or
even amassing a tidy sum. Someone's sum is always tidier.
Sure, I could make something of myself, but the fact is, every
time I meet a self-made man, I walk away thinking somebody else could have done a better job.

I've even cut way back on reflex actions. After examining
me, doctors pound themselves with their mallets. It goes
back to birth, when they resorted to luring me out with Her-
shey bars. Mother was pushing, I was pulling. After all, how
often do you find a place with all the amenities included?
Finally, it was the tong wars. To this day, I have a fear of
icemen.

All of this means that I'm physically incapable of being
anything other than self-employed—and even so, suffer from
a high rate of absenteeism I've been meaning to speak to
myself about.

**Consuela started buying me
chipped beef because the
president eats it. This
morning she crumbled a
Butterfinger onto my Team
flakes. I'm afraid she has
political aspirations for me.**

Confessions of a Workavoidic

I'm a workavoidic, the flip side of the workaholic coin. Maynard G. Krebs is my patron saint. In order to work at all, I have to trick myself into thinking it's a game. This goes back to my first job at Auto Parts and Service, Inc., where I spent the best part of a working day hiding from the muffler moguls in the tailpipe bin. Needless to say, by the end of the day I was exhausted.

Workavoidics are the paranoids of physical effort. We think people are out to get us to work. And, what's worse, for them. Workavoidics are idealistic: The notion of working for "superiors" flies in the face of our democratic ideals. It's not that we're too good to work, it's that we're not good enough. A guidance counselor (who, I realize now, was a closet workavoidic) once diagnosed me as a perfectionist who couldn't deal with the sloppy work I produced. And it's true: Torn with conflict in the workplace, I feel compelled to take the afternoon off and snake the toilet.

Being around feverish activity brings out the torpor in me. Beehives of activity give me hives. I identify with the worker who sets his own pace, particularly if it's leisurely. When I see a guy leaning on a shovel, I want to go over and prop him up with a two-by-four and shake his hand. Ronald Reagan had the right idea: five hours a day in the saddle, tops. Any more and you'll end up being tied to it.

I've thought about forming a support group for workavoidics, but it doesn't seem worth the effort. Instead, I've put together some tips for fence-sitters who really would like to be sloughing off but haven't gotten around to it. I call these "The Four Shortcuts":

1. *Delegate authority. All of it, if possible.*

2. *Avoid pressing concerns unless your pants are involved.*

3. *Use your time efficiently. Take a working lunch and eat as much of your paperwork as possible. Keep in mind the paperless workplace is a stepping-stone to the workless workplace.*

4. *If you must work, remember that work equals force times distance. Take a little work and make it go a long way.*

Remember, no one ever got rich through hard work. If you insist on working hard, you do so at your own economic peril.

An avid skier I
know has the
bumper sticker
"Pray for Nuclear
Winter."

Where There's Smoke There's Ire

Feeling a natural affinity for neurotic behavior, I'm sympathetic to smokers. I don't know why, but I generally find smokers to be more interesting than nonsmokers; maybe it's the gesturing or the hunted look they have about them. I guess I'd rather air out my sweater than listen to someone rattle on about what he doesn't do. (I know what they're saying about secondhand smoke, but it's a secondhand sweater.) You've got to feel for the middle-aged middle manager who, at the apogee of his career arc, has to stand in the parking lot in subzero weather to catch a smoke. Especially since once he goes inside they may be asking for his urine.

They banned smoking in our workplace. Now there's so much smoke in the men's room a lot of guys bring hams to cure. It's not hard to tell the displaced smokers walking around. They're the ones chewing gum like it was cud—the ones who don't have St. Vitus dance, they just really need something to do with their hands. Some of the women are twirling batons, and one guy took up the lariat. And if he lassos the Xerox girl once more, it's Smokers Anonymous for him. Then there are the ones who obviously need something to suck on. You know, middle management. It doesn't help esprit de corps to see your supervisor toking on an executive binky. Some have gone to filters. No cigarettes, just filters.

One guy tried lettuce cigarettes but kept leaving little pellets around the halls. Then there's the cosmetic approach some smokers are taking—you know, yellow Lee Press-On nails and a little liquid smoke behind each ear. Technology hasn't really provided any answers, although smokeless cigarettes did seem like just the thing after safe sex.

The warnings on the packs are pretty bad—cancer, high blood pressure, heart disease, pregnancy risk—and those are just the lights. But if they ban advertising entirely, it's only going to put more cowboys out of work. How are we going to know which women have come a long way? And with the reaction against chewing tobacco, how are ballplayers going to get that lump look in the dugout? Silicone implants, sure, but they travel. Watching those guys spit is bad enough without seeing them eject sunflower shells like spent cartridges (and on dugout steps, too: an accident waiting to happen).

I'm afraid the antismoking campaign may be selectively breeding a tougher type of smoker, guys who wouldn't hesitate to strike a match on the bridge of your nose should you suggest it might not be a good idea to light up around the oxygen tent. Women driven to dens of sin just because they're not smoke-free environments. After all, when smoking is outlawed, only outlaws will smoke—and they're going to look a lot tougher than cops chewing sugarless gum.

I'm Mike, Fly Me!

taught high school in the seventies, when the approved manual was *Teaching as a Subversive Activity*. I got my big break in Kenosha, Wisconsin, when the previous intern was seen at the country-club welcome in sandals and sent scuttling. During my interview, I was asked if I would be sitting cross-legged in a lotus posture on my desk while teaching. At the time I really thought I wouldn't, and got the job. Driving down from Madison that first day, I saw smoke rising from Tremper High School and thought the revolution had beat me down I-94. Turned out to be Senior Bratwurst Day.

Teacher training neglects one of the fundamental areas of classroom knowledge, how to break a hammerlock. If you can't break a hammerlock at the start of the semester, they'll pin you all year long. Humor, of course, went a long way with my students, although eventually they got tired of laughing at me and we got down to business, group discussions of their parents' personal problems. (Turned out that's where a lot of them learned their hammerlocks.) My being Jewish was a source of wonder to many of them, since—at the time—I was not the balding owner of an appliance store. I still don't own an appliance store. Although openness was the watchword, I must admit the constant "values clarification" got on my nerves. Finally, when it came to deciding who would enter the fallout shelter in the event of nuclear war, I remember recommending the priest, the scientist, and the historian all be left outside, and we just take the show girl, a few ugly but good-natured guys, and a deck of cards.

I encouraged my students to call me Mike, whether they wanted to or not. Some begged to call me Mr. Feldman, but I felt we had to get tough if we were going to pull this Aquarian thing off. And discussions, lots of discussions. We had so many discussions we had discussion backlash ("This is supposed to be English class, not Discussion class." Needless to say, we talked about it.) Each day we put all the desks in a circle and each night the custodian moved them back into rows. (The Postulate of Euclid really is "You can't sweep a circle." Nick Euclid, Custodian.) Although the administration wouldn't go for a classroom without walls (something about "structural integrity"), they did let us paint Mayan borders around the ones we had. Once you have Mayan walls, it's a small step to remove the desks altogether, and let the students bring in beanbag chairs and sofas, which we did, the educational theory being if you're going to sleep at your seat, why not be comfortable? (Desks, if you recall, hit you right here and cut off the circulation.)

My peers did not all accept me with open arms, even when I tried to integrate myself into the lounge huddles of the social studies teachers/coaches, whose conversations were mostly audibles called on the line. I always imagined these guys teaching the Nazi invasion of Poland as "First down for Hitler." Nary a one wanted to hear about Joyce Carol Oates, despite her deep love of boxing. The behavior in teachers' lounges, by the way, is just what you have always suspected: rowdy and boisterous, with spitballs and an occasional mock chicken leg flying, until a student knocks and timidly sticks his or her head in the door. Then they're perfect angels.

Having seen *Blackboard Jungle*, I never brought in my priceless collection of 78s, although, in retrospect, I apologize for all the Simon and Garfunkel. Maybe he wasn't a poet. And making them blindfold one another and often as not be led into the opposite-sex lavatory, what was that? And Shakespeare? O.K., you were right, he was stupid.

Never read him anymore. If nothing else, teaching is the perfect antidote to graduate school. After a mere decade or so, my vocabulary is even beginning to grow back in. After the teachers' lounge I never thought it would. My own aside, I never really had many discipline problems. It's a cliché, I guess, but some of the toughest kids turned out to be some of the toughest, and some of the most likable turned out to be some of the most likable. Once they came to accept you, there was really nothing they wouldn't do for you, particularly if it involved parts from a Cutlass. It goes to show, book learning isn't everything.

 Then there's the classic underachiever who broke into the school's computer system and changed all his grades to Bs.

Radio Free Me

God did not give me a radio voice. Table legs, but not a radio voice. I don't have a diaphragm or something. My tones are banana shaped. In connection with me, when "voice" is the noun, "nasal" is most often the modifier. My saving grace is a dysfunction that compels me to free-associate under stress. Until radio, it was a liability. For years, I thought my name was Enough Already. I don't know what I'd do if it weren't for radio—probably shout on the street that Santa is an anagram for Satan, or sit in the bus station tearing articles out of newspapers with one eye on the public-address mike.

Radio is therapeutic. Not so much for the listeners (who can't be helped) but for the people on it. I suffered postdivorce trauma, postadolescent miasma, and turning forty on the air, all at the expense of my listeners, a cherished radio tradition. Many called and said they hoped I'd never get well. I strongly recommend radio therapy, particularly if you can get yourself a call-in show. It makes you feel better just knowing how many people out there are as bad off or worse.

I never had legitimate training for the career, not that there is any. In high school I won a guest DJ contest and was told by the real jock the secret was to not talk so much—good advice for him. I had actually forgotten about radio entirely until I stumbled onto it by volunteering at a local radio station (listener-sponsored WORT, home of the Wortniks), during my annual Christmas depression. (Years later I would meet my second wife on Christmas and finally have a basis for the feeling, actually a premonition.) My big break was a couple of years' broadcasting from Dolly's Fine

Food in Madison (it was food; how fine depended a lot on what you, the eater, brought to it), annoying people while they ate. It was like being home again. Although I brought those skills and more acquired while teaching (speaking to an imaginary audience) and driving a cab (using a mike while groping for something) to public radio, I was not immediately taken to the bosom and nursed by the highbrows in it, although I'll hold my expanse of forehead to any in the business. (You can't talk to people who have classical music as their mission, though, especially if you've only had one semester of music appreciation and *A Night on Bald Mountain* is not playing.) My only commercial experience was two weekend overnights on a local rock station (where a young woman, at two in the morning, requested "Hell's Bells" by AC/DC for her newborn niece), and a career that ran for the worst part of a year at WGN in Chicago, where, as an experiment, I was paired with a woman who was the incarnation of a mental block.

I enjoy what I do while I'm doing it, although afterward I have my doubts, along with everybody else, as well as the guilt generated from continually having to explain what I do the rest of the week, the same question people wouldn't dream of asking their priest, rabbi, or pastor. (I know, because I play pinochle with them.) Radio brought me out of myself, and I'll be damned if I can stuff it back in. Having a live audience is a great way to meet people, since you generally never see them again, the exception being the unfortunate woman in the audience I married, a true violation of the Broadcasting Code of Ethics. People are generally quite receptive and absolutely forthcoming in letting me know that I'm all wrong—I'm too short, I'm too tall, I'm not that ugly, or I've got "a face made for radio" (everyone seems to think they made that one up), I'm really not all that bald, etc., etc. Just what someone who obviously craves reassurance or he wouldn't be in the business wants to hear. The medium is an inexact science; if I tell people I'm six four and blond, that may not be literally true, but maybe it is in a more important sense. Maybe there's a Schwartzenegger buried deep inside of me, and a Maria Shriver waiting at home. You don't know. So turn me in to Accuracy in Media.

Of course, people do think they know you, and I'm starting to think maybe they're right. When you're spewing out the cartridges of your life, you don't really expect people to pocket the shell casings, but they do. It seems as if I must have revealed everything on air except my wife's hair color, which she forbids me to do. Otherwise, she doesn't mind what I say about her on radio nearly as much as the very same things said in the friendly confines. So, if I'm feeling witty at her expense, I try to do it through a door. (But no longer the front one. She can lock that.) Generally, that's not the problem people think it must be; she likes being mythological, and I'd prefer her to be. Besides, Consuela is not merely my wife, she is every woman I have never known, as I tried to explain to the storm door the other day.

Well, I'll have to wait until Saturday.

Dad loved Mickey
Spillane. I was the
only kid in grade
school who knew
a great set of
gams when he
saw them.

A Red Letterman Day

You probably missed my Letterman appearance, coming, as it did, right at the end of the show after several unsuccessful illusions by Kamar, the Discount Magician. I nearly missed it myself, since they left me sitting in the hotel lobby right up to showtime, pulling up my carefully selected socks (kind of expressionist black-and-white—I got a lot of good feedback on them) and thinking about what my brother Arthur (Letterman's biggest fan) told me about their leaving guests to sit in the hotel when they decide they don't really want you. ("Sometimes they'll leave you there for several days, and then just send you home.") I even thought it might be God's wrath, since this was the first night of Rosh Hashanah (we entered Manhattan upstream in an exodus of Lincoln Town Cars), but as it turned out, they merely forgot me. Besides, God would understand: This was Letterman.

I had been pre-interviewed by the segment producer, and so no longer had anything to say about any of my agreed-upon possible areas: life in the Midwest, the un-wacky world of public radio, the joint-custody-of-frozen-embryos case, and middle-aged fatherhood. What Dave would call "boffo stuff," particularly compared to Ann Archer's meager offering of riveting beauty and struggles with Gene Hackman on top of a moving train. (She was good, but she completely lacked what I like to call "pedestrian quality.") "Hit the chair running," the segment producer told me, as I waited behind the set for Kamar, who was having difficulty removing a sword from the throat of the talent coordinator. "Remember to let Dave lead you," said the producer, coming up to us. "I thought I was supposed to hit the chair running,"

I said. "That's right," said the segment producer, "hit the chair running and let Dave lead you. Whatever you do, don't let Dave lose interest, or he'll start to bail out and you don't want that." "No," I said. It seemed like a lot of responsibility, though, a guest trying to make the host comfortable.

I entered after a gentle prod from the floor director, and everything went swimmingly until I made the turn around the guest chairs on the set (to shake Dave's hand) and very nearly hit the chair sprawling when my pivot foot went out from under me. (Leather soles. In all the concern about socks, I didn't think through shoes.) Fortunately, Dave was there for me. I was so happy not to have fallen that when I sat down, I just smiled. Dave looked concerned, flipped my card, and asked the difference between American and National Public Radio. Something clicked: It was the collective sound of ten million TV sets.

Just for the record, since you say you didn't have a chance to see it, here is the synopsis of my Letterman appearance. On the Midwest: "Decent values and a Jew can still make a good living"; on any confusion in the public mind between myself and Garrison Keillor: "I get it all the time, the height, the Norwegian thing. . . ." On frozen embryos: "Dear, did you remember to fill the embryo tray?" which segued to our impending birth: "We're doing it the old-fashioned way—in the oven." Dave was making an involuntary bailing motion with his coffee cup as we went to break, but did actually lean over to me (which I'm told does not very often happen) and say, "I was in Madison once—in January." "Nice timing," I said.

Afterward, while they combed the RCA building for my driver (who forgot to pick me up in the first place), I watched Dave leave in his Ball State cap and sweatshirt, football tucked under his arm, and Paul Schaeffer commiserate with the blond page in the hall where Kamar sprayed his blade with Pam.

The genuine Late Night® T-shirt I sent to Arthur, who said I looked nervous. "Nice socks, though."

If You Want to Be a Badger, Come Along with Me

Part Five

Yes, I am from around here (Milwaukee). No, I'm not from New York. What in tarnation gave you that idea?

Lived here all my life, with the exception of a brief stint

somewhat short of a career in Chicago, and one summer which nearly stretched into a fall in Boulder at the Naropa Institute, where I crashed trying to transcend.

I like Wisconsin because it's casual. We stand on informality. You don't have to say "Come as you are" around here, because people already have, and brought a hot tuna dish to boot (besides, it would be "Come by as you are," anyway). My wardrobe works in a place where people have an everyday parka and one for formal occasions (the dark knit caps are worn after seven, although crushables can turn up anytime). People in Wisconsin are nice to you when they don't have to be, like on the phone, at the checkout, and in traffic, where horns are rarely used because you might see the guy later and there's no point in starting bad blood. Should you founder on an icy street, which, face it, happens, the people who quickly surround your vehicle are much more likely to push you out than demand your valuables. Besides, what do they need with another parka? They've already got two.

The Bush transportation plan is revealed—hop in the car and drive. This is hard on the heels of the Bush savings plan—put the money in the bank and live off the interest—and the Bush education plan—divide the school day into seven periods, each devoted to a different subject.

Ich Bin Ein Milwaukeean

There are those who say jaywalking cannot be curbed. Let them come to Milwaukee! There are those who would have us believe that lawn care cannot be a way of life. Let them come to Milwaukee! There are those who do not know the difference between a bubbler and a water fountain, and God knows where they've been soaking their feet—let them come to Milwaukee! Yes, my friends, I am proud to say, "Ich bin ein Milwaukeean!"

THE AUTHOR, *pandering to Milwaukeeans*

They say you can't go home again. You can, but you discover they've put green siding on it. I'm not kidding; our old house looks like a record-breaking avocado. When I think all of the times I risked a heart attack watching Dad go up on that three-story ladder to paint it tan. The cement-block retaining wall he built—The Great Wall of Dave Feldman—looks like Joshua's been there. That was a great wall, too—you could crouch behind it and rain snowballs (plaguelike) on Uptown Motors across the alley with near-complete impunity. The object was to see if you could startle the salesmen into dropping their feet off their desks and running out into the lot long enough for you to slip in and grab the keys to a sharp-looking Hudson fastback. We never got that far, but a guy could dream.

The alley's even in disrepair, if an alley can be in disrepair. I don't know, I've never seen a new one. That alley was
the world to me—playground, escape route, toboggan slide.
With proper icing, you could sled all the way from Fifty-
eight Street to Ruth's Sweet Shop on Fifty-first, knocking
Rabbi Twerski off his feet on Fifty-third if you cut it too
close to sunset. But if you got past Twerski, it was a round
of wax lips for everybody.

I didn't knock on the door. I was afraid we still lived there
and I'd be back in the damn bedroom with Arthur, my Mori-
arty, trying to sleep in the beds Dad built in without benefit
of box springs. I used to pool up at night like a blob of mercury. Arthur in those days was some kind of nematode, a
night creature that came up from the basement (where, generally, he had been converting my bike into a golf cart, or
failing in an attempt to make my six-transistor radio into a
two-transistor radio) to bed only in the wee hours, flipping
on the light and whistling while he filed between his toes
with his sweat sock. The upside was that my bad dreams, by
comparison, didn't seem so bad. There were actually worse
accommodations in the house: Howard slept in the sun-
room, which was on Highway 41. An amazing number of cattle moved past our house. We felt like the only Jews on the
Santa Fe trail.

Mother was the only one who liked the house. With all
those strings of lights over the used-car lots, she didn't have
to put on the kitchen light. And it was convenient; in winter,
Barger's bakery was only a black-and-blue fall and swollen
knee down the alley which, unfortunately, we had iced that
day for a new try at the record: all the way down to Sher-
man Park at Forty-third Street. (Never, to my knowledge,
been done, although Mom came the closest.)

A Hunter's Guide

The opening of deer season in Wisconsin threatens to bring a record number of commodities brokers, corporate attorneys, and RV salesmen to Wisconsin's north woods to work out the frustrations of their respective professions, leaving behind a half million wives to work out theirs. While a man needs no special training to stalk game, since hunting skill is locked into the male genetic code, many who will be escaping to Wisconsin over the next nine days will be novices. For the aspiring Nimrod who, in anticipation of bagging his first whitetail, has already purchased a very large bag, here are some pointers:

1. You will need a gun of some sort. If you grab the flintlock over the mantelpiece, make sure the hammer has not been soldered. With a doe bearing down on you full tilt, it's one hell of a time to discover you're carrying an ornament. If you don't have a gun, try looking through the back pages of *Soldier of Fortune* magazine for one that appeals to you. Many have found the AK-47 or the Uzi to be a good all-climate choice. Whatever you choose, remember the first rule of the hunt: Keep your weapon clean. More than one prize fawn has been lost when a dirty action has caused the hunter to miss his quarry and strike a neighbor's chimney. Break your gun down nightly, and soak it in a light-duty oil, such as safflower, and garnish to taste. During those long nights in the chilly cabin, clean your bore often.

2. Bring along some scent. You're not alone in the woods, you know, and a week is a long time to try to get by on your good looks. Deer urine is the scent of choice of many old-timers, while Opium is favored by younger sportsmen.

3. Carry a call. A hunter should at all times carry a full complement of calls suitably arrayed bandido style on crossed ammo belts. A useful selection includes an adjustable goose, a pintail, a high-volume diving duck, Snort Deer, a gobble box, a split-reed raspy yelp, and an elk call with a detachable grunt tube. While most of these will never be used outside the Tomahawk Tap, it will at least let everyone at the bar know you're ready for anything, sheepshead included.

4. Don't expect game to come right out in the open and greet you. Mammals are shy and surprisingly reluctant to run up to guys in orange vests smelling like deer urine. Furthermore, deer are masters of disguise: The figure you see in the Groucho nose and glasses may be a futures trader from Glencoe and it may not. If there's any doubt, aim for the attaché case.

5. Speaking of which, don't be embarrassed to carry a bag. Many of the new "possibles" bags look like ladies' purses, but since you will be armed, it's highly unlikely anyone will say anything. To lessen the possibility of sartorial self-consciousness, however, pack a single strand of pearls.

6. Carry a decoy. If it looks enough like you, the warden may haul *it* off.

7. Should you bag a deer, let it hang from the basketball hoop on the garage as a warning to the neighbors. You'll want to give away as many of the steaks and chops as possible, since no matter how often you call it "venison," everybody knows it's still "deer meat." Make sure you find someone reputable to process it. If, after eating your sausage, you find yourself scratching behind your ear with your leg, the sausage maker may have substituted other cuts.

8. Finally, after using your tracking skills to find your way home after a week, all hollow-eyed, irritable, and empty-handed, to a wife who looks curiously rested and who, at least for the first couple of days, sings around the house in a pleasant voice you don't recall her having, ask no questions.

▼

Then I'm working on a Milwaukee version of *Driving Miss Daisy* called "Driving Miss Gerry," wherein my mother becomes friendly with the black driver on the Center Street bus. (He gives her extra time on the transfer, drops her at unmarked corners, chats with her despite the "no visiting with driver" signs.) Dad notices something's up when she begins cooking chitlins for several days, trying to explain them away as kishkes.

Gardeners
Anonymous

I belonged to Gardeners Anonymous. Whenever I feel the urge to break the soil, I call a number and a horticulturist rushes over to tie me to the trellis. You see, I have a black thumb. I'm an Israeli in reverse: I turn gardens into deserts.

I mean well: I like tilling, I like sowing, and I thoroughly enjoy reaping. It's tending I don't have the time for. I think it's presumptuous to interfere with nature. As I understand natural selection, the peas are supposed to fend for themselves, and with pluck and tenacity, the best get to be Birdseye.

In 1970, when Canned Heat said it was time to be "goin' up the country," I did so, with my mail-order bride, several packets of Northrup King seeds, and a copy of *The Whole Earth Catalog* for the privy. The marriage faltered, but the beans flourished: wax beans, butter beans, Chinese pod beans . . . it never occurred to me that getting back to the earth meant I was going to have to eat my beans. After the first three-bean salad, I began to have misgivings. Perhaps the sons of accountants would not inherit the earth.

Fortunately, it was the height of the resurgence in the primitive arts in America, and I discovered that beans gone to seed—has-beans—produce very attractive agatelike seeds, which an enterprising young fellow might string on a little elastic and sell to unsuspecting returning alumni on the library mall on campus. I was that young fellow. Meanwhile, back up the country, the wife was mummifying pickles and putting up preserves where I couldn't reach them. We were that close to our dream of being self-sufficient: We were insufficient.

Naturally, nature had the last laugh. Not only did those strung beans sprout on many an old grad's environmentally ideal neck, but that harvest was my last bumper crop. Now my corn gets the blight, my wheat the smut, and my garbanzos the wilt. I get rootworms that would've stopped Alex Haley, and the slugs just drink my beer bait and stagger on to ever greater destruction.

One year I planted potatoes and forgot where. Another time, I had a vigorous tomato plant, but it was on the compost heap. For three months I gave succor to a weed impersonating rhubarb. I tried planting fish, like the Indians, but none grew. Sowing naked by the light of the full moon proved to be of no avail; the neighbors merely moved their patio parties indoors.

Still, when the frost starts to come out of the ground, I can't help but feel that old fierce pull of the soil, and I long once again to walk barefoot over the furrowed fields of my youth, breaking clods of dirt beneath my toes despite the real possibility of trichinosis. Then I remembered my childhood was nothing like that, and reach for the phone.

Self-What?

During the past year, shuttling between home and Burbank on show business (the Disney people claimed they could animate me), what struck me were the surprising similarities between Los Angeles and Wisconsin, often referred to, after all, as "the Third Coast." Aaron Spelling's house and the state capitol in Madison, for example: Seen side by side, you'd be hard pressed to pick which was the house "jiggle" built. We have teardowns like they do in Beverly Hills, too, where small mansions are demolished to build bigger ones. Ours generally result in metal pole barns, but they sure are a darn sight better than the sheds that were (barely) standing there before.

Nor are we immune from the social ills found in a metropolis like Los Angeles: drive-bys are quite common in Wisconsin, although we call them come-bys, since people generally just roll down the window and threaten to come by the house later. Like the gangs in L.A., a lot of guys around Wausau have taken to wearing red or blue plaid shirts and house slippers, although their range of hand signals ("left-turn," "right-turn," and "go-around, we're talking") is admittedly more limited. Graffiti splashed across Wisconsin garage doors, tableaus of whitetails or trout leaping at flies, makes it pretty clear whose turf you're on. Air quality can be a problem, too, particularly when a low cloud cover rolling in off Lake Michigan pushes the eau de Usinger's Sausage back down over Milwaukee, resulting in one of a number of "kielbasa warning days" during the summer when Jews and Muslims are advised to stay indoors. Traffic is no picnic these days, either, what with the tillers on the road in the spring and the corn pickers in the fall. Passing two lanes of gleaming stainless-steel teeth is not unlike looking around the table at a breakfast meeting with producers and entertainment lawyers in Santa Monica.

Even film crews are becoming commonplace in Wisconsin, particularly when Milwaukee's striking resemblance to Cleveland or Kenosha's to Gdansk is crucial to the story line. We're all on pins and needles waiting for the Lech Walesa story to happen. And although we don't have the same number of celebrities on the street that you'll find in Hollywood (just Bob Uecker, actually, and he can't be everywhere), we do have people who look so much like a Burt Reynolds or a Pia Zadora that you want to hop off the bus and ask them what they're doing walking into the Harnischfeger manufacturing plant with a lunch bucket. (Researching a role?) Here, of course, you don't have to be a star to get your footprints in cement, you just have to wait until the crew knocks off for the day.

One thing we don't have in Wisconsin, however, is a commission on self-esteem. The legislature in Sacramento a couple of years ago established the California Commission on Self-Esteem to ask the big question: Can you be packed in yeast, wrapped in seaweed, and sprayed from helicopters and still have self-esteem? (It's enough to send you in early for your 30,000-mile brain tune-up!) Sure, we take yeast here in Wisconsin, but internally, the way nature intended. We never even got around to walking on coals, except accidentally, after a tailgate party at Green Bay's Lambeau Field (and then it wasn't exactly a mantra that was recited). Californians are different in these respects. They'll jump off bridges wearing nothing but bungee cords, but are afraid to drink their tap water. In fact, they react to someone drinking tap water the way we would to a dog drinking from the toilet. That's why the Perrier scare didn't hit us like it did them: Most of our bottled water goes into the iron. We want pristine water, we get it from when the earth was young, up around La Crosse, made into a complete food with hops and barley.

We tried to form a Self-Esteem Commission here in Wisconsin, but no one felt qualified. You don't want people to think you're better than everyone else. (We have a Republican governor—he wanted to start a Self-Interest Commission, but no one would cooperate.) If we did have a Self-Esteem Commission, I doubt it would be capitalized. Why draw attention to it? Its recommendations would be a foregone conclusion: sheepshead and a glass of beer, Dungeons and Dragons and a glass of beer for the younger set, and for stubborn cases, cribbage. If all else fails, Bingo at the Ho Chunk Reservation Hall. If that doesn't work, you may have untreatable self-esteem and be happier in California.

The pendulum
swings: In my
neighborhood
artist's spaces are
being converted
into empty
warehouses.

He's Not Heavy, He's from Brodhead

More Wisconsin people admit they're fat than do people anywhere else in the country: 25.7 percent. Instead of scoring points for candor, we're taking a lot of ribbing—or would be, if they could get at them. North Dakota used to be the fattest, but they stopped owning up to it about the time they toyed with dropping the "North" so they'd sound warmer. Well, what can you do, they have the missiles.

At least nobody here in the nation's certified midsection is losing any weight over it. What with some population loss in the census, we're pretty happy our total mass is holding steady. On balance, if we're anything, it's not too fat, it's too friendly: When a guy at the mall (and he must be from around here with that rear end) carrying a clipboard (with no checks clamped in it) stops us and asks if we have a minute, we're not going to lie, even if the nachos start to set up some. Anyway, sometimes they give you coupons for Cheez-Whiz for answering. So, yes, we could stand to lose a few, who couldn't?

Next thing you know, a front page spinning like a propeller stops to reveal the headline "America's Fattyland," complete with a picture from behind of the self-same couple from the mall who, granted, had no business wearing shorts anyway. Then *USA Today* splashes a three-color graphic of the state as an oven mitt pulling a casserole out of Canada across their fold, along with a sausage bar graph showing Wisconsin as the whole kielbasa.

What the surveys don't measure are large bones. A lot of us in Wisconsin are large-boned. That's the price you pay for wonderful personalities. Put large bones together, you get big frames, the better with which to see the big picture. The Native Americans who were here, the French, the Germans, and the Scandinavians who came, all had one thing in common: big frames. When they saw other people with big frames, they knew they were in the right place. A big frame can carry weight, and what it can't goes into an Oshkosh B'Gosh, anyway. In fact, you probably wouldn't have known it was in there at all if you hadn't asked. Unless, of course, you're one of those outside fatgitators.

Japanese Kobe beef
is selling here for a
hundred dollars for
an eight-ounce
portion. A guy could
grind it and give his
wife a meatball
necklace.

The Cheese Plate

It may be a moo point now, but I mourn the passing of the cheese plate. True, as a license, it wasn't really edible, and it sometimes made me feel like I had a "kick me" sign bolted to my bumpers as I wandered Indiana or looked for my friend in Pennsylvania, but that was a small price to pay to show your true colors, Colby yellow and Holstein black. Sure, "America's Dairyland" reinforced the still widely held belief that there are more cows than people in Wisconsin, but that's only because they're encouraged to breed.

Now we've got plates that look dangerously like those of Illinois. It's getting so you don't know who to resent anymore on I-94. I recently tailgated a guy for six or seven miles before I got close enough to see he was one of us. It's a generic catchall of a license, with a sailboat, a barn, and what looks like either Gumby or a zucchini in between. The incongruity is bound to scare off tourists; all that's missing is a muskie leaping out of a milk pail. The worst thing about them is they're white, and don't even come with a tablet of orange dye like the oleo we were forced to consume for so many years. They're a setback. It's hard to imagine a convict taking pride in stamping out one of these.

Personally, I don't hold with what I see as dairy denial. For me, cows have never stopped being exotic, kind of like land manatees. Growing up in God's country, Milwaukee, I believed that if you crossed a Golden Gurnsey with a Holstein, you got a Goldstein. I see no reason to change my opinion now. The cows that stood along the Class B highways on our forays to the four corners of Wisconsin beckoned me like bovine sirens in an alfalfa sea. When I learn they were domestic animals, I vowed never to marry unless she had spots on her sides.

To this day, in my more serene moments, I can see myself nestled deep in the bosom of Dairyland, living alone in a little bungalow built for two, a dog roasting on the hearth, an apple tree just outside the window, and a stream running past the door, with cows in it, worrying the trout. And, in the foreground, an aqua and white Rambler Classic with cheese plates, now, unfortunately, expired.

An increasing
number of young
people today are
signing predating
agreements which, in
the event they break
up, clarify disposition
of concert tickets.

What You Should Know

- -

Part Six

There have been—or there has been (which is it?)—a glut of books published recently about cultural literacy. If you said "have," you probably haven't read any of them, have ("has"?) you. That's the trouble with books on cultural literacy: Surprisingly few cultural illiterates pick them up, unless it's to prop open a window. Not that you are an illiterate—on the contrary, you're reading this, aren't you? The fact is you've had a good education: the broad overviews, the surveys, symposiums, the teas hosted by teaching assistants, the in-depth looks-at, even three credits of earth science, for God's sake, so you can dazzle some passing oil-company geologist with a pointed reference to chert. Nor, I might add, is this storehouse purely academic: Over the years you've gained an understanding of the mound system, which some day may do you some good, and you've certainly learned enough in the school of hard knocks to know you prefer the soft ones.

But, let's face it, there are no Cliff's notes for life. You can't breeze through this one and cram for the final. You are expected—by co-workers, social acquaintances, and business contacts (although not by spouses, thank God) to sound like you know a few things so they can continue to give you the benefit of the doubt. Maybe you won't come up with enough insights to write a book about how stupid everybody else is and then sell it to them (the perfect literary crime), but if you can pull the wool over even one pair of eyes—particularly bespectacled—it can really get you through your day. Perhaps your thirst for knowledge for appearance's sake will lead you, as mine has, to the opening of the thousand-petaled index-card file attained in transcending to the elevated state of *quizmaster*. Think of it, the man with all the answers—because he wrote the questions.

Like [sic] this "Instant Cultural Literacy" test you're about to take—I got a hundred on it! You will, too, eventually, if you keep at it. By that time the references, survey results, cross-cultural insights, strong backgrounds in academic disciplines, and tiny cocktail wieners of wisdom should catapult you right over the heads of those who struggle in vain to place the name "Grendel." Here's how the quiz works: Read each question and try to give the right answer. Check, and, if you're wrong, try it again. Try it as many times as you like until you finally get it. When you do, that's one right. When you get them all right, *you* will be all right (at least in my book), and need never be a pariah at another party (unless it's a party of pariahs), for you will have something to contribute. Or you could bring a dish to pass.

People

In a crowd of a hundred people, how many can play the clarinet?
7. Even worse, 11 can play the organ, and 33 claim to be singer-songwriters.

What percent of American women do not own a pair of jeans?
(a) 5%   (b) 16%   *(c) 27%

How big is the average man's head?
*(a) 7¼   (b) 7⅜   (c) 7½
Although around here he wears an adjustable seed cap, so it's moot.

How many American kids expect their parents to buy them a car as soon as they're old enough to drive?
(a) ⅓   *(b) ½   (c) All
And it had better be red.

How many women say buying a swimsuit is traumatic?
(a) 1 in 4   *(b) 1 in 3   (c) 1 in 2
Men don't have this problem since women buy their swimsuits.

How much more often are boys called on in school than girls?
*(a) 8 times   (b) 10 times   (c) 20 times
Usually preceded by "Mr. . . ." Not a serious attempt at eliciting information.

According to the "Wisconsin Trout Angler Studies," how many other fishermen would an angler like to see on a fishing trip?
(a) The more the merrier

    (b) One or two, tops
   *(c) None
They don't go out in the middle of the night in the middle
of nowhere for nothing, or, rather, they do.

Who changes their underpants the most, the French or the Germans?

The French, 56% to 45%. The Spaniards are the unsung
underpants heroes of the Common Market at a 59% rate.

When asked at Disney World, "Have you ever bounced a check?," visitors from which part of the country were most likely to refuse to answer?

   *(a) Midwest (15%)
    (b) South (13%)
    (c) Northeast (12%)
We're not saying we have, and we're not saying we
haven't.

According to the National Geographic Society survey, how many Americans (out of 10) think the United States is part of the Warsaw Pact?

   *(a) 1   (b) 3   (c) 5
Around here, a slightly higher number think we're part of
the Wausau Pact. But that's around here.

How many Brits admit being more attached to their pets than their spouses?

    (a) 1 in 5   *(b) 1 in 10   (c) 1 in 20
One in five like them better than their kids. The majority
would rather socialize with a pet than another Englishman.

Do people goof off more in groups or when alone?

In groups, although more are totally comatose alone

Most shoplifters are caught:

    (a) On a Friday in June
   *(b) On a Wednesday in January
    (c) On a Monday in September
Most are men; most conceal items in their purses. Go
figure.

According to a Vanderbilt psychologist, 80% of women have cried at work. What percent of men have?
   (a) .085%   (b) 12%   *(c) 50%

And more of the men cry because they are "emotionally moved." So there.

What percent of people in American families make a real effort to eat vegetables in the cabbage family?
   (a) 11%   (b) 29%   *(c) 65%

Are people more loyal to their mayonnaise or their coffee?

Mayo—65% to 58% for coffee. Only 29% are loyal to their battery.

According to bartenders, bartenders leave the best tips. Who leaves the worst?

Doctors. Followed by lawyers, bankers, and teachers. Other good tippers include waitpersons, tavern owners, and beauticians.

What percent of Americans would sacrifice a finger for a big part in a movie?

5%, according to a WCBS poll in New York City

14% of American pet owners have sent their pets postcards while on vacation. What percent have talked to their pets on the phone?

57%

Do more men or women mind their manners when they're with their spouses?

Men, 62% to 56%, at least according to each

What percent of American high school seniors think the Panama Canal saves sailing time between New York and London?

16%

Which causes anxiety to more people—going to a party of your spouse's co-workers, or being asked about your hemorrhoids on the bus?

74% say the party situation would cause them anxiety; 65% cite a personal question asked in public.

Out of 4 Americans, how many prefer bad art to the masters?
3. The other one's couch just happens to match a Renoir.

What percent of adults 18 to 29 played charades last year?
(a) 5%   (b) 12%   *(c) 22%
This, according to Gallup, is the peak age group for charades, falling off to 1% in the over-fifties.

When told not to peek at something, 100% of 3-year-olds did. What percent admitted it?
(a) 10%   (b) 25%   *(c) 40%

Who are better sleepers, men or women?
Women. Men are disturbed ten to forty times per night; women are disturbed only by men.

The number-one complaint drivers make about other drivers is:
Being tailgated. No turn signals, being cut off, and driving too slowly follow.

What percent of Americans say they have many acquaintances but few close friends?
70%

Would more men like to change their teeth or their thighs?
Teeth, 36% to 9%. You hardly ever hear a guy talking about his thighs.

What percentage of teenage girls use a deodorant?
99%, according to Daniel Evan Weiss in *One Hundred Percent American*

What percentage of men think buying a wedding gift is as bad as going to the dentist?
21%. The worst is buying a wedding gift for a dentist.

According to *Celebrity Plus* magazine, how many Americans think "First Lady" should be a Cabinet position?

10%. Whether or not she should run on the same ticket as the president was not asked.

According to researchers at the State University of New York-Albany, if you'd like to stay happily married, should you spend more money on big-ticket items (appliances, durable goods, homes) or small-ticket items (stereos, TVs, sporting equipment)?

Big. Happily marrieds tend to spend more on items that are less easily divisible.

If you haven't completed high school you are:
    (a) As likely
    (b) Twice as likely
  *(c) Four times as likely
    as high school graduates to watch home-shopping television

Who drinks more beer than Wisconsinites?
  *(a) New Hampshirites
    (b) Texans
    (c) No one

In New Hampshire they guzzle 35.7 gallons per year to our 32.1.

What percentage of Americans who smoke don't want to stop?

7%

According to personnel directors, which is the most productive day of the week?

Tuesday. Which might explain why Tuesday night is a working woman's least favorite night to have sex.

What percent of second graders believe the earth is round?

5%. 40% of third graders do, 55% of fourth, and 75% of fifth. It then falls off again in middle age, when everything else is round.

Do teens prefer French or Japanese food?

French, 3% to 2%

According to *USA Today,* Americans think what percent of their friends will go to Hell?
25%. 72% think their own chances of going to Heaven are good or excellent.

In 1967 82.9% of college freshmen were looking for "a meaningful philosophy of life." What percent were in 1987?
39%, according to the American Council on Education

A woman gains 18 pounds during the first 13 years of marriage. Does that mean she's happy?
Yes. An unhappy married woman gains 43 pounds.

Who vacuums more, the oldest son or the oldest daughter?
The oldest son, 21% to 20%

According to the Gallup poll, which M&M is least likely to be eaten first?
The yellow

What percent of nurses want to marry doctors?
20%, according to the *S.F. Chronicle*. The rest go into it for the bad hours.

According to the Kohler Company, households with one bathroom suffer how many times more bathroom stress than those with two or more bathrooms?
4 times

Have more adults in British Columbia or in Saskatchewan had sex with a member of the opposite sex?
British Columbia, 93% to 81% in Saskatchewan, despite the inviting wheat fields

Are more Americans interested in ballroom dancing or in vegetarianism?
Ballroom dancing, 26% to 18%

Out of ten bald Iowans, how many think bald men are more attractive?
4

According to the California poll, women admit more dishonest behavior than men in which category?
>   (a) Calling in sick when they're not
>   (b) Removing towels from a motel
> *(c) None

Which means either that men are more honest or women are. (Includes keeping change, taking work supplies, exam cheating, shoplifting.)

According to the Epcot poll, what percent of adults visiting Walt Disney World think compassion is the number-one attribute for a president?
> 3% (men 4%, women 2%). Donald could run and win.

What percent of the readers of *Philip Morris Magazine* smoke after sex?
> 53%

Places

Which is considered rude in Korea, burping or blowing your nose?
The latter. Burping means compliments to the chef.

In England, when you order "lights," what do you get?
Beef lungs

How many outhouses are there on 20,302-foot Mount McKinley?
    (a) none   *(b) 2   (c) 1
They're planning a third, though, at 17,000 feet. Until then, climbers are asked to take waste and place it in crevasses.

When you arrive at a home in Ghana after the dinner hour, should you expect to be fed?
Yes. The extended family includes extended hours. The Frugal Gourmet, on the other hand, expects you to be there on time.

What color do brides wear in China?
    (a) White   (b) Black   *(c) Red
White at funerals

How many pages of Andersons are there in the Stockholm phone book?
    *(a) 48   (b) 76   (c) 101
And 378,000 Johansons

What's the dollar called in Singapore?
The dollar

In Cincinnati Four-Way Chili, what's under the chili, cheese, and onions?
Spaghetti

If Durante were saying good night to Mrs. Calabash in South Carolina, who would he be saying good night to?
The wife of a turtle cooked in the shell, "wherever you are"

Which state was, for a short time, the "Brainpower State"?
Minnesota, but they took down the sign (on I-94, just across the line from Hudson, Wisconsin).

Which has a higher percentage of sunshine in February, Milwaukee or Cleveland?
Milwaukee, 47% to 37%. So El Paso has 82%, big deal.

The only Jackalope you can ride can be found at what well-known stop in South Dakota?
Wall Drug

Bonnyclabber to a New Englander looks a lot like what to the rest of us?
Cottage cheese

How many cars are there in Florida for every ten people?
12. 12.8 million residents, 15.1 million cars. Some cars do not, apparently, have residents.

How many sing-a-long rooms are there in Japan?
12,000. Also there are 800 phone clubs, where you can make crank calls to someone on the premises.

The Maharishi Mahesh Yogi is building the City of Immortals, his vision of heaven on earth, where?
Oklahoma

How many Keillors are there in the Copenhagen phone book?
None

Which state's motto is "Si quaeris peninsulam amoenam, circumspice," "If you seek a pleasant peninsula, look about you"?
Michigan

Everybody knows noodles were brought to Italy from China. Was rice brought to China from Italy?

Yes

Were more people bitten by penguins or lionfish in New York City in 1987?
Lionfish, 2 bites to 1. 72 gerbil bites, though

Is gas more expensive in Prague or the Ivory Coast?
Prague—$5.46 per gallon, Ivory Coast—$4.04 per gallon. Cheapest: Venezuela, 43¢ per gallon.

In what state will you find "johnny cakes," snail salad, and the Chowder Dome?
Rhode Island

According to a Wendy's salad-bar survey, what region of the country uses the most black olives?
The West

Do Swedes like crayfish?
Like 'em? They love 'em, importing over a thousand tons per year.

Routine procedures can be speeded up in Egypt with a little *baksheesh.* **What is it?**
A tip or a bribe, depending upon whether you're receiving or giving

The House of Representatives in Tennessee proclaimed the second week in May "Official Goo Goo Week." What's an Official Goo Goo?
According to the proclamation: "A luscious combination of creamy marshmallow, chewy caramel, roasted peanuts, and pure milk chocolate." And they're round, besides.

Where are you most likely to be hit by an uninsured motorist?
   *(a) Washington, D.C.
    (b) Mississippi
    (c) Iowa

In the West, if you are "boss simple," what are you?
Intimidated by your employer

Is a Danish pastry Danish?

No, the first danish showed up in Jewish bakeries in New York City. Just sounds better than a "prune Jewish."

Where might you sidle up to a bowl of callaloo soup with a side of coocoo?

Trinidad, Jamaica, Haiti

In Pennsylvania Dutch country, *vas is schnitz*?

Dried apples, usually served with *knepp*

What percent of Iowans who own birds would like them to be more affectionate?

57%. 30% would like their cats to be more affectionate, and 40% their fish.

Is Milwaukee or San Jose better for your complexion?

Milwaukee, due to lack of harmful sunrays. Other good cities: Seattle, Cleveland, Cincinnati, Columbus, and Portland. Avoid Phoenix.

True or False: There is a law in France that permits the government to veto your first name.

True. As decreed by Napoleon, the state demands that children be named only after religious and historical figures. Silly first names are prosecutable.

What seafood delicacy do Detroit Redwings fans throw onto the ice?

Octopuses, symbolic of the eight tentacles, or games, needed to win the Stanley Cup

When people across the United States were asked which states made up the Midwest, they could agree on only one. Which one?

Iowa

When invited to an Egyptian home, should you feel free to stick your nose into every room?

Yes. If you don't, they'll feel hurt.

For a cup of coffee and a piece of pie in Tokyo they get:
13 dollars. And no refills.

Which of the following states is least stressful?
  *(a) Kansas   (b) Idaho   (c) Nirvana
Nevada, Georgia, and Alaska were ranked most stressful.

When the swallows leave Capistrano, where do they go?
Argentina

"Mexican caviar" is:
  (a) Blowfish eyes
  *(b) Waterfly larvae
  (c) Crab eggs
Big in the western state of Michoacán

Can you buy dental floss in London on a Sunday?
No, but you can get partly cooked tripe.

In Lagos, Nigeria, what's a "go-slow"?
Traffic jam

True or False: Lafayette Park, across from the White House, has cannibalistic squirrels.
True, due to what is thought to be the highest squirrel density in the world, 160 per 7 acres

A Saudi kisses you on the nose. Call that an apology?
Yes

Jousting is the official sport of what state?
Maryland

How many bars are there in Parliament?
8. And many more barristers at them.

According to an *L.A. Times* poll, how many drivers in Los Angeles out of ten have made indecent gestures while driving?
4. 1 in 10 got out and mixed it up.

What percentage of working women in Iowa are primarily responsible for lawn care?

7%. 3% are the ones to see for home repairs.

Are you more likely to call a pancake a "batter cake" in Georgia or Pennsylvania?
Georgia, and throughout the South. Who calls them flapjacks we won't know until Frederic Cassidy comes out with the next volume of his *Dictionary of American Regional English.*

What do they get for a parking space on Beacon Hill in Boston?
$135,000

True or False: Wisconsin is considering random drug testing for cows.
True—for bovine growth hormone. Some cows have been pumping up with it.

Can you eat your pet in California?
No, not as of January 1, 1991, when it became illegal to eat anything "commonly kept as a pet or companion."

According to its tourist ads, which of the following is "the land of love, bounty, growth and freedom to witness the horizons of ingenious creativity consecrating the society of happiness and bounty"?
(a) Lebanon   (b) Northern Ireland   *(c) Libya

According to the census, what percentage of the people in New Jersey live in metropolitan areas?
100%. New York: 90%, Wisconsin: 66.5%, and Idaho: 19.6%

Denver has the lowest per capita consumption of prune juice in the United States. Which city has the highest?
That's right, Miami

Things You Should Have Learned in School (Had You Been Paying Attention)

Who said, "When I use a word, it means just what I choose it to mean, neither more nor less"?
Humpty Dumpty, as told to Bill Moyers

What's the "vermi-" in *vermicelli*?
Worms

Which line segment is longer, A–B, or C–D?
They're the same size.

What does it mean to "cross one's Rubicon"?
To take an irrevocable step, such as attacking Pompey

Is a note passed in class constitutionally protected speech under the First Amendment?
Apparently not

All you have to do is force a dyne one centimeter and you've got an:
Erg (the centimeter-gram-second unit of work)

How do you spell "license" as in "license applied for"?
And the "s" goes this way.

Why did Prometheus get his liver gnawed?
He stole fire (and eventually had his liver cooked).

Illustrate peristalsis using only a mongoose and a rat.
Good

If there's no "panacea," what is it there isn't?
A remedy for whatever ails you

Why did Thoreau eat a woodchuck?
To make Emerson Thoreau-up

If you've got movement of your fluid through your permeable membrane, what have you got?
Osmosis

What are the following: "Overcrowding in Guppies," "How do Guinea Pigs Respond to Sensory Deprivation?," and "The World in a Drop of Sewer Water"?
Science projects. You know, for the Science Fair.

When you think "Polish astronomer," you probably think:
Copernicus, who thought the world revolved around Galileo

Who wrote the following?
A child should always say what's true
And speak when he is spoken to,
And behave mannerly at table;
At least as far as he is able.

Robert Louis Stevenson in *A Child's Garden of Verses.*
Adults neglect to mention the second couplet.

What is a petri dish?
A dish prepared by Laura for Rob. Also a dish containing a
medium for growing laboratory cultures

**Name the one home ec/shop project that held up over the
years.**
The wooden Kleenex box

How much is a "plethora"?
Too

"Look on my works ye mighty and _____?"
". . . despair." Either "Ozymandius" or "Ozzyharrietus"

Who's got cotyledons?
Beans do.

What's a "flying buttress"?
Women's wear designed by Howard Hughes. Either that
or the masonry arches supporting the walls of Gothic
cathedrals and allowing them to rise to great heights.

**"Put your lips together and blow" (Lauren Bacall) is really a
description of what scientific principle?**
Bernoulli's. You do know how to create a partial vacuum,
don't you?

**What's wrong with the following? "All penguins are black
and white. Jim is wearing black and white. Therefore, Jim is
a penguin?"**
It has an undistributed middle, as does Jim.

**Let's say you commit a crime so original they have to invent
a law for it. Continuing the tribute, they decide to prosecute
you. Why can't they?**
The Constitution forbids such *ex post facto* laws.

If a steering wheel were a clock, what time would it be?

Ten to two if your left arm is longer, ten after eleven if your right is

You'd most probably use your _____ to detect a "miasma."
Nose. "The noxious exhalations from putrescent matter."

What Roman god forever united medicine and thievery?
Mercury (the former Hermes), who also dabbled in commerce, speechmaking, and floral deliveries

What kind of beetle did Gregor Samsa awake to find himself one morning?
A dung beetle. Scarier still, he used to wake up as a civil servant.

What were the two sides in the French and Indian War?
The French and the Indians versus the British

What's the little flappy thing called that guards your windpipe?
Epiglottis

The ancient practice of using birds as fortune cookies is called:
Augury

The Moving Finger, having writ, does what?
Moves on. "Nor all thy piety nor wit/Shall lure it back to cancel half a line . . ." Edward FitzGerald, *The Rubáiyát of Omar Khayyám*

What's Esperanto?
The Romance-based world language that no one speaks

The "supermundane" is:
Above and beyond that which is found in school

Give one example where a low coefficient of friction is your friend.

Demonstrate a squat thrust.

Are grade A eggs best?

No, AA

What is the "denouement"?
Where *Great Expectations* finally ends (plot resolution)

Is the management responsible for Articles of Confederation left in the room?
No. Nor constitutions, either.

What's supposed to happen in the Id?
Your instincts, so don't worry about it.

The four tastes are:
Sweet, sour, salt, and acquired, er, bitter

If you had one problem noted consistently on your report card it was: _____ (fill in).

What's the difference between a permeable and a semipermeable membrane?
One must be clogged or something.

Can the school psychologist commit you?
No, and the counselor can't counsel you.

What's an "idyll," anyway?
A narrative poem. That's where the guy keeps talking.

To his Roman friends Hermes is known as:
Mercury

Should you excuse yourself after an "eructation"?
I should say so (burp).

In chemistry, what's a retort?
A distilling vessel

What is it again when there's a word or group of words between "to" and its accompanying verb form, as in "to formally object"?
A split infinitive

In language lab, how do you know when the teacher's listening?

You don't.

At what point do the formation of the Lutheran church and invertebrate zoology coincide?
The Diet of Worms

What stone marker was discovered in 1799 that provided the key to deciphering hieroglyphics.
The Donna, er, Rosetta stone. Had the same message in Greek and Egyptian script.

In the event of nuclear war, what is the proper "duck and cover" procedure?
Get your outer garments, proceed single file, no talking, to the basement, and kneel facing the wall with your parka over your head. Wait for further instructions.

If you've got "rectitude," what have you got?
Moral virtue. Unfortunately, you can't really brag about it.

Is "shilly-shally" an antonym or a synonym for "dilly-dally"?
Synonym (to dawdle, undecided)

The style of art and literature developed principally in the twentieth century which stresses the subconscious or nonrational significance of imagery arrived at through the random exploration of unexpected juxtapositions is called *surrealism*, or, another day, another dollar.

Simplifying the scorecard of ancient tribes of the British Isles, the Picts merged with what other well-known tribe?
The Scots

"Vacation Bible School" is an example of:
    (a) Onomatopoeia
  *(b) An oxymoron
    (c) A parenthetical expression

If "ziggurats" are not Babylonian smokes, what are they?
The terraced pyramids from whence hung the gardens

Zipangu was the name given what country by Marco Polo?
Japan. What they called him is not recorded.

What were the skeptics skeptical about?
You name it. And with good reason, since they believed real knowledge can't be had.

If Rome had been named after Romulus's brother, what would it have been called?
Reme

When you flummox somebody, what have you done?
Confused them, but good

Why—when a student enters the teachers' lounge—does everybody stop talking?
Whom do you think they were talking about?

What do you call canals in the ear that are partly round?
Semicircular canals

In dodgeball, the object is to:
    *(a) Hit the guy
    *(b) Hit the guy where it hurts
    *(c) Hit the guy where it hurts, hard

If you're either a pedestal table or two profiles nose to nose, what kind of a relationship have you got?
Figure-ground

Is "pons" a part of the brain or a character in *The Tempest*?
The brain. It's the bridge on top of the medulla oblongata.

The sirens that supposedly lured sailors to their deaths were actually:
    *(a) Bull walruses with nice voices
    (b) Water spouts
    (c) Hallucinations caused by fermented rye bread

Science

According to the *Atlantic Monthly,* how long will it be before *The Twilight Zone* reaches parts of the Milky Way where audiences untouched by network TV might exist?
  *(a) 1,000 years (b) 10,000 years (c) 50,000 years

Can elephant seals nap while diving?
  Yes, according to Professor Le Boeuf at the University of California-Santa Cruz, who has discovered them asleep at the seal

True or False: "Love" is located in the "reptilian" or primitive section of the human brain.
  True, according to psychologist Joseph Wolpe, who also notes that this is "the same part of the brain which makes sharks go into a feeding frenzy"

It sounds silly, but can an electric-eel–skin wallet demagnetize your credit cards?
  Yes, according to the Steinhart Aquarium in San Francisco

When it belongs to a piece of steak we call it gristle, when it belongs to us we call it _____?
  Cartilage

The sky's the limit in the exciting new field of exopsychology. What is it?
  The study of the behavior and attitudes of extraterrestrials, particularly those involved in cattle mutilations

Do bees have tiny little mental maps or do they navigate by landmarks?

Maps. So why can't Consuela use one?

A half-sized slinky walks down stairs
    (a) Half as fast   (b) As fast   *(c) Twice as fast
as a full-sized one

What is misleading about the so-called three-toed woodpecker?
    It has six toes.

How many fat cells are there in the human body?
    (a) As many as there are cells
    *(b) 30 billion
    (c) 100 billion
According to Rockefeller University in New York, "They are not distributed evenly."

Could I be telling the truth when I say I'm allergic to exercise?
    Yes. The thought of it can cause hives, choking, a drop in blood pressure, and loss of consciousness.

According to a University of Vermont scientist, what's the secret to laying low-cholestoral eggs?
    *(a) Be a hen and eat fish oil
    (b) Be a hen and mate with a prairie chicken
    (c) Be a hen with your nest at 10,000 feet above sea level

By the end of a five-hour picnic, the salmonella count in the potato salad will have increased:
    (a)   10 fold   (b)   100 fold   *(c) 1,000 fold
It doubles about every half hour.

With names like up, down, strange, charm, truth, and beauty, they must either have been born during the summer of love or be _____?
    Quarks

Do plants cry?
    Yes, particularly when they sense a vegetarian. Drought-

stricken plants emit high-pitched screams in the 100-kilohertz range.

Are human teeth getting bigger or smaller?
Smaller and in my case, fewer as well. They've shrunk 50% in the last 100,000 years.

According to Einstein, "the most important tool of the theoretical physicist is his _____"
(a) Sense of humor   *(b) Waste basket   (c) Swiss army knife

Primate evolution around here led to Ed, my neighbor who collects tires. What did it lead to in Madagascar?
The lemur, including the only recently discovered Greater Bamboo Lemur

True or False: Antiperspirants work by clogging the pores.
False. We sweat when positively charged pores pull at negatively charged droplets of sweat. Aluminum present in anti-perspirants reverses the positive pores to negative.

True or False: Paleontologists in France have discovered a Cro-Magnon skull with dental bridgework very similar to what I've got here.
False. The earliest dental plan goes back to the Bronze Age, the Shang dynasty in China. Their false teeth still fit after 3,000 years.

Who or what is the *Turdus migratorius*?
Robin redbreast

A beaver and a camel are friends. Which is likelier to attend the other's funeral?
The camel, who can expect to live to twenty-five, the last ten without his little friend. The real question is how they met.

Are people mostly white meat or dark meat?
Dark meat, according to Professor Robert Baker of Cornell's Poultry Science department (who knows his

featherless bipeds as well). The dark color is due to the
abundance of myoglobin, the iron pigment that stores
oxygen in muscles.

**Would an alligator repellent most likely be derived from the
glands near the tail of the alligator or those under its jaw?**
    Jaw. Wear the tail scent and you may find yourself in a
short but passionate relationship.

Do scallops have 42 blue eyes, 42 brown eyes, or 21 of each?
    42 Old Blue Eyes

Does Mantovani aid or hinder digestion?
    According to Johns Hopkins, Mantovani is a digestion aid.

**Can you expect a striped garter snake to freeze or flee when
poked?**
    Flee. The stripes make it difficult for a predator (or a mere
annoyer, like you) to judge its speed. Your mottled garter
snakes tend to freeze.

**What's a hundred and twenty million years old and comes in
either green drab or beige?**
    The world's oldest flower, discovered in Australia: the
fossil koonwana plant, a kind of wild yam

Do spiral seashells go the other way south of the equator?
    No

**What percent of methane in the atmosphere comes from
livestock?**
    15%, a little more than half of that from belching

**The most recent scientific data suggest the center of the
Milky Way is:**
    *(a) Football shaped
    (b) Pear shaped
    (c) Made of nougat

A mosquito, when coddled, can live how long?
    (a) A month   *(b) 5 months   (c) 8 months

When the wind's kicking up on Neptune's Great Dark Spot, how high does she kick?
1,500 mph, the record in the Cosmos outside of Chicago's Loop in January

Oh, yes, it's the Great Attractor. What is it?
A concentration of galaxies and matter so large that astronomers totally overlooked it. It attracts entire continents of galaxies at the rate of 400 miles per second.

Which is edible, the monarch or viceroy butterfly?
The viceroy. Its defense is that it looks like the monarch, which contains toxins compounded from milkweed-pod resins.

Do female vampire bats have a mutual-support system?
Yes (according to Gerald Wilkinson in *Scientific American*). The females can live as long as 18 years and maintain friendships for nearly their entire lives with other females, while the males come and go.

Were a Neanderthal couple the same height as my parents?
Yes. Dad: five feet five, Mom: four feet eleven

Name the personal-use concoction which is made of acid, soap, shortening, castor oil, wax, fish scales, perfume, dye, and ammonia.
Lipstick

How many pounces does it take for a cat to subdue a rabbit?
5. 2 to 4.4 for a rodent, 3 for the average invertebrate

Who's faster, a dragonfly or a hornet?
A dragonfly, who can zip along at up to 25 mph. A hornet can go 12, while a housefly (which, granted, has other nice qualities) lollygags at 5 mph.

The brain: It's about time, it's about space. Which half is about which?
Left: time, right: space

According to the University of Toronto low-cholesterol diet, you should snack:

(a)   3 times a day
(b) 10 times a day
*(c) 17 times a day
Subjects lowered their cholesterol levels 13.5%.

True or False: Scientists at Temple University have produced DNA strands using amino acids found in hair conditioner.
False

True or False: Earwax is a key to cardiovascular diseases, breast cancer, and arteriosclerosis, as well as a marker of racial origin.
True, according to Victor Spitsin, Soviet biologist, and father of earwax classification (dry and wet, Estonian and Ukranian, etc.). Protein content tells all.

Is pollen boys or girls?
Boys

Why do pigs root up truffles?
They contain a compound nearly identical to a sex attractant found in sows.

Yes, Siamese fighting fish yawn before fighting, or no, they don't.
Yes, according to Ronald Baenninger at Temple University, although the fight could be a yawner.

The adrenal glands ride shotgun on what organs?
The kidneys

Is Krazy Glue good for patching holes in corneas?
Yes, according to Dr. Thomas John, at Michael Reese in Chicago. Afterward, you'll feel like hanging from your hard hat at a construction site.

If the universe starts to shrink instead of expand, would time run backward?
No, but your clothes might fit. Dr. Stephen Hawking of Cambridge used to think it would, but he's changed his

mind. Time would run forward, he now says, but people could no longer exist.

What is the difference between matter and antimatter?
They are mirror images of each other but have opposite electrical charges. Brought together they would annihilate one another, a process seen elsewhere in nature only in marriage.

If your mouth twists to one side as your head is cocked, you are expressing the one human emotion revealed asymmetrically on the face. Is it:
(a) Fear   *(b) Contempt   (c) Surprise
This was the expression with which some researchers greeted the University of California-San Francisco findings.

Odds 'n' Ends

What is the highest form of life struck down by an extraterrestrial object?
    (a) A pigeon from Secaucus, N.J.
   *(b) An Egyptian dog
    (c) A rose bush in Lima, Peru
In 1911, "Nalchla" was struck down by a meteorite.

Shirley Temple sat in how many laps as a child?
   *(a) 200   (b) 500   (c) 1,000
The most comfortable? J. Edgar Hoover's.

According to teenage singing sensation Tiffany, which came first, she or Tiffany lamps?
    She did. "Tiffany lamps came out when I was about ten."

What is a "key grip" in charge of on a movie set?
   *(a) The guys who do all the shlepping
    (b) The guys who do the electrical work
    (c) The keys

Which of the following tastes like fried pork rinds?
   *(a) White worms   (b) Beetles   (c) Wasps
Beetles taste like apples, wasps like pine nuts, and your red worms are hot and spicy.

In Hawaii, the literal meaning of this stringed instrument is "flea" and not (surprisingly) "flee." What is it?
    The ukulele

Is a hybrid between a swan and a goose called a "swoose" or a "g'wan"?
    A swoose

Hamlet* is the number-three best-selling Cliff's Notes, *Macbeth

the number-two. What is the all-time Cliff's best seller?
   (a) *Silas Marner*
   (b) *A Tale of Two Cities*
   *(c) *The Scarlet Letter*

A police officer dealing with teenagers should:
   (a) Ask them if they're holding up the wall
   *(b) Establish two-way communication with them
   (c) Tell them about seeing Roy Orbison at the Iowa State Fair in 1965

True or False: The frantic Italian dance, the tarantella, originated when someone was bitten on a dance floor in Palermo.
   False, although the bite of the tarantula was supposed to cause the type of dancing which this dance cured

The Zamboni machine is used to:
   (a) Make bagels
   *(b) Resurface ice
   (c) Align wheels
Invented by Frank Zamboni—over 4,000 are use in 32 countries.

If you mail a concrete block, will the Post Office deliver it?
   Yes, and the cement, too, providing the postage is correct. A man in Alaska had his entire house mailed into the wilderness, and is now looking for a mail-order bride.

When a bureaucrat is parameterizing, what the heck is he doing?
   Setting limits

If it's not the current crop of nurses, what's a "nurse crop"?
   A crop planted with another to minimize weeds, e.g., corn planted with aspens.

In a deck of cards, what's the "puppy foot"?
   The ace of clubs

If a "Dutch barn" is a barn without sides, what's a "Dutch cheese"?

Baldness. A "Dutch auction" starts with the highest bid and works down.

True or False: "Tawdry" is short for St. Audrey.
True. Not Audrey herself so much, but St. Audrey's Fair, where one could find an abundance of showy or gaudy lace.

The physical malformation "hooker's elbow" comes from what practice?
Excessive ice fishing

David Holland, dog jeweler, recommends which of the following for a male retriever?
   (a) 18K gold necklace
 *(b) A heavy silver-link necklace
   (c) A simple strand of pearls
"They walk differently. They sit up straighter."

Was Milli Vanilli one person or two?
Four. Rimsky-Korsakov was one.

What is a circa 1930 Babe Ruth candy wrapper worth today?
   (a) $100   (b) $1,000   *(c) $10,000
According to Barry Halper of Edison, New Jersey, who seems to have the only one

As a Junior Miss contestant (1976, Georgia), Deborah Norville listed which pair as "Current Personalities of Interest"?
 *(a) Anita Bryant and Princess Grace
   (b) Gloria Steinem and Jackson Browne
   (c) Rosalynn Carter and Joe Namath

A new zipper that alerts the wearer of the pants his/her fly is open does so using:
   (a) Heat   (b) Sound   *(c) Vibration

What percent of food products introduced in 1989 bore health claims?
   (a) 30%   *(b) 40%   (c) 50%

What are the odds your wrong number will be to a fax machine?
  *(a) 1 in 39   (b) 1 in 56   (c) 1 in 100

How many pucks do they go through in an average NHL game?
  (a) A dozen   (b) 20   *(c) 40

May an Orthodox Jew receive an organ (transplant) from a pig?
  Yes, as long as he doesn't nosh on it

A gap in your front teeth of 2mm or more qualifies you for membership in what national organization?
  The Diastemic Club of America

How long did a '77 Monte Carlo run without oil or water at the fair in Ladysmith, Wisconsin?
  (a) It didn't
  *(b) 2:03
  (c) Nearly 6 minutes

At what age does a child begin to use pronouns indiscriminately?
  *(a) 24 months   (b) 30 months   (c) 36 months
  By 30 months they pretty much have settled on "me."

Was Fornax the Roman goddess of physical gratification or baking?
  Baking, although for many the two are intertwined. Fornacalia comes up in February.

The four categories, according to experts, an hourglass, pear, inverted triangle, and rectangle are categories of what?
  Women's figures. Men's go from here to here.

Which is higher, The Right Reverend Monsignor or the Very Reverend Monsignor?
  The former. It's like olives.

According to campaign parlance, a candidate can have Big Mo, Little Mo, or No Mo. What's Mo?
Momentum. Also, Whad'ya Mo?

A photomaniac has an abnormal desire for?
Daylight

True or False: Alice Cooper bought his first car from Evan Mecham.
True

If you're "woaded," what are you?
Colored blue

The tradition of playing "Hail to the Chief" when the president enters the room began when which president's entrances went unnoticed once too often?
James Polk's. His wife ordered it.

According to Cornell, do chickens prefer Vivaldi's or Frankie Valli's *Four Seasons*?
Vivaldi's. They do like "Big Hens Don't Cry," though.

Built according to biblical specs, what would Noah's ark set you back today?
$165,944.08, according to Scott Fisher, estimator at Williams Lumber in Rhinebeck, N.Y. He figured $13.00 a cubit.

Which of the following celebrities lives in a home made of tires and aluminum cans held together with mortar?
   (a) Victoria Principal
  *(b) Dennis Weaver
   (c) Frank Zappa
The three-story, 6,500-square-foot hideaway in Ridgeway, Colorado, took 3,500 tires and 20,000 cans to complete.

How long should you allow for the roasting of an ox?
3 days, although my mother would leave it in for seven, easy

The sackbut was a medieval musical instrument someone had the good sense to rename the:
Trombone

True or False: The (snappy) patter of a comedian is a term coming from the Paternoster, the Lord's Prayer.
True, according to Robert Claiborne (*Word Mysteries and Histories*). *Patter* referred to prayers recited rapidly and insincerely.

A "belly builder":
    (a) Works on the hulls of wooden ships
 *(b) Assembles the innards of pianos
    (c) Works on essentially the same principles as the "Abdominizer"

Where would you find "Venus's flower basket"?
Next to Adonis's bed. Also off the Philippines and Japan; it's a sponge.

How many mosquitoes do Off's biting-insect people go through in a six-week period?
A million

According to Asae Shichi at Oakland University, which of the following should be avoided when doing business with the Japanese?
    (a) Sports   (b) Small talk   *(c) World War II.
Also, do remember to look at everybody's business cards.

How long does it take to replace a toenail?
Depends on if it's in stock. Otherwise 6 to 8 months (only one-third as fast as fingernails).

What does it mean to "carry straws" for someone?
To court; you know, like the birdies do

Do British butchers sire more male children than British nonbutchers?
Yes—121 per 100 daughters, compared to the national average 105.6 per 100

According to the *Jobs Rated Almanac*, who has the worst working environment, school-bus drivers or astronauts?
Astronauts. They step outside to smoke, they implode.

According to Hugh Hefner, the bunny symbol for *Playboy* came from:
    (a) A drawing made by one of the younger girls he was dating
   *(b) The design on his blankee
    (c) A caricature of a nun he made while at St. Mark's

How many fingers did John the Baptist have?
50 at last count, according to the total number of sacred relics said to be his fingers. Saint Stephen has 13 arms and Saint Agatha 5 breasts.

Which of the following is not an opening line recommended by Barbara Walters in an interview?
    (a) If a fairy godmother offered you 3 wishes, what would you ask for?
    (b) What was the toughest time in your life?
   *(c) Did you ever feel like your undies were riding up your crotch and there was nothing you could do about it?

How much does Queen Elizabeth pay for a brassiere?
   (a) £19.95   (b) £29.95   *(c) $570.00
At Rigby and Peller. Her waist cincher runs about $720.